How Long
Will They
Mourn Me?

How Long Will They Mourn Me?

The Life and Legacy of Tupac Shakur

An unauthorized biography
Candace Sandy and
Dawn Marie Daniels

ONE WORLD
BALLANTINE BOOKS · NEW YORK

2006 One World Mass Market Edition

Copyright © 2006 by Random House, Inc.

Published in the United States by One World Books, an imprint of The Random House Publishing Group, a division of Random House, Inc., New York.

ONE WORLD is a registered trademark and the One World colophon is a trademark of Random House, Inc.

ISBN: 0-345-49483-0

Cover illustration: © Heather Mckay

Printed in the United States of America

www.oneworldbooks.net

OPM   9 8 7 6 5 4 3 2 1

Acknowledgments

We would like to thank an extraordinary team that helped make this book possible: Melody Guy and Danielle Durkin from Random House, Congressman Gregory W. Meeks and Simone-Marie Meeks and staff, Mom and Dad, and the Samuel, Hamlet and Fraley families. Thanks to Ann Brown, Joella Irving, and Chanel Skyers.

Gwendolyn Quinn and Robyn Ryland-Sanders and the Black Public Relations Collective, Jelani Bandele Octavia Bostick, Denise Hidden Beach, Katrina Boswell, Bill Carpenter, Ronda Carson, Lisa Chase-Patterson, Dee Dee Cocheta-Williams, Lisa Knox, Eric Moore, Jackie O, and Tonya Payton.

Alithia Alleyne, Cristy Colon, Maggie and James Goring, VP Records, Selina Johnson, Rachia Hazel, Curtis Taylor, Ursula Miller, The Wax, Ronnie Wright, and Arnold Turner.

Contents

PROLOGUE
Death Around the Corner

Even though I'm marked for death,
I'm a spark till I lose my breath.
—TUPAC SHAKUR

Some say rap is a new form of black exploitation, weaving the theme of death systematically through hundreds of songs, as they engross a generation through music videos while reassuring them that violence is all right. If you went out in a hail of bullets, like a ghetto soldier or the idolized characters in movies like *Scarface, The Godfather,* and *Heat,* you became a ghetto legend. But are any of us truly aware of when our lives will slip away? Did Tupac Amaru Shakur know about his impending death? Gangsta rap and its stars first made a fortune from stories of drugs, drive-bys, the code of money, power, and respect. The partying, women, and sex was inevitably followed by the glorified death of another brother on the streets, but only they knew what was going on in our hood—America didn't care unless it crossed the invisible line.

In the movie *Heat,* the lead character played by Robert De Niro states, "Never get attached to anything that you cannot walk away from in thirty seconds or less." That is the code for the streets; movie clips become codes by which street hustlers live and die. It becomes easier this way, when you take out rival gang members who may have played Matchbox cars with you in elementary school. Murder was justice exacted for deals gone bad, turf taken, and respect not given.

The media coldly and analytically report just another murder, but the streets create an insider folklore legend celebrated on neighborhood corners, on stoops, and in jailhouses for the fast, colorful life the victims lived. While through this urban legendry they ultimately get the respect they always yearned for in life, their families and loved ones are torn apart.

Glorifying death and the gangsta lifestyle through music had become popular among various rappers such as NWA (Niggaz With Attitude), Ice T, Bone Thugs and Harmony, Biggie Smalls, and Snoop Dogg. But Tupac's lyrics have stayed with us much longer, as if haunting a generation who witnessed his life unfold. One has to wonder whether he was a prophet or an eerie example of life imitating art.

Tupac Shakur's art was expressed through love letters to his people, whom he intimately understood and appreciated for the realness they were experiencing. On one side were the broken down and disenfranchised who succumbed to the system, and on the other were the rebels of the underground who were tired of living this hell on earth and were ready to fight. His music shared his lessons learned, his request for forgiveness, his impending death, and warnings to victims of revenge. He asked what would happen in "If I Die 2 Night?", a song featured on both *Me Against the World* and *Tupac's Greatest Hits*:

And I hope I'm forgiven for Thug Livin when I die
I wonder if heaven got a ghetto for Thug niggaz

*Headlines readin MURDERED TO DEATH, my
last breath
Take a look picture a crook on his last stand
Motherfuckers don't understand, if I die tonight*

It depicts a man ready to stop worrying about what happens next; he wants to be given peace as he takes his last breath. His legacy unfolds as a headline on a daily newspaper: "Murdered to Death." Many of the producers who worked with Tupac said he often expressed whatever was on his mind that day in the studio. Was Tupac exercising the same philosophy about death and its glorification, which has become part of the life in the hood?

Death to the young and black in America is a normal and expected occurrence. The *New York Times* reported that in certain communities, death is looked forward to—that "children in grammar schools prepare what they will wear at their funerals in advance." It left Tupac to wonder out loud through song if heaven has a ghetto:

*Let the Lord judge the criminals
If I die, I wonder if heaven got a ghetto.*

What would you do if you knew you were going to die? How would you handle the news? Would you give up? Would you fight? Would you dare to dream though the odds seemed stacked against you?

No one really knows if Tupac Amaru Shakur knew he was going to die young. Many who knew him have said he felt he was a marked man. As fans of his music and silent observers of his life, we can only speculate that this sense of impending death contributed to his meteoric rise. At the time of his death at the young age of twenty-five, Tupac had more goals he wanted to accomplish. Many can attest that he accomplished those goals tenfold and more.

Like a not-so-subtle birthmark, was death the ever-present factor that gave Tupac his search for deeper meaning in a seemingly hopeless America for a young black man? Whether he felt he was marked for death because of his heritage, because he was the son of a Black Panther and godson of the persecuted and con-victed Black Panthers Assata Shakur (also known as Joanne Chesimard) and Geronimo Pratt, or because he was a young black man in a society that gave up on black men before they were born, we will never know. Tupac grew during a time of evolutionary change for black people, surrounded by the revolutionaries who so desired to create social and economic change by any means necessary. Watching his mother—his role model—struggle because she, too, was marked by the government for her belief in equality for people of color in some sense made Tupac a sacrifice to that rev-olution. Was his drive born out of this struggle, as well as his sense of impending doom?

Some speculate that what could have been his obses-sion with death presented itself later. Perhaps it was driven by his many direct confrontations with the police—from his first beating by the police in Oakland in 1991 to his shooting of two police officers in Atlanta in 1993. Having such a great and public dissension with an army in blue across the country could make anyone paranoid, let alone feel he had a bull's-eye on his back wherever he went. An atmosphere of mistrust can drive one to want to push beyond the constraints of society, both physically and mentally.

Many admirers of Tupac's music trace his transition and the evolution of his fixation with mortality in his lyrics and through his films. From the jovial lyrics of Digital Underground to his first solo album *2Pacalypse Now,* you can see the development of his independence and his individual persona.

As he matured, Tupac seemingly struggled with two sides of his personality: the self-destructive, me-against-the-world Tupac and the caring, I-want-to-change-the-world Tupac. John Leland of *Newsweek* reported that, "In recent interviews, he talked about two identities fighting inside him. 'One wants to live in peace, and the other won't die unless he's free.' The split could be maddening. He rhymed moving tributes to black women, and to his mother; he rhymed about bitches and hos. He spun tales of gratuitous carnage; he talked about the need for education and black self-sufficiency. He was indestructible; he was uncommonly vulnerable. He was the most articulate voice of intelligent black male anger. The split was not Tupac's alone, and it was part of the blood that bound him to the community." Even professionally, he made a spilt—2Pac for music, Tupac for his acting credits. It seems even he realized there were dual Tupacs running parallel. Now, one can only speculate whether the two sparring sides of Tupac ever would have found a happy medium, maintaining his revolutionary spirit while nurturing his scholarly nature. A constant public battle raged between the hardcore, reckless T.H.U.G. L.I.F.E. Tupac and the sensitive Tupac who cared about the injustices of the world, as demonstrated in songs like "Brenda Had a Baby" and the ode to his mother, "Dear Mama." There was no happy medium; instead, it seemed there were indeed two Tupacs squaring off with each other as the young man's fragile life teetered on destruction. Yet, ten years after his death, Tupac's music, his message, his activism, and influence still have a place in the souls of young people, from the streets of America to the villages of Peru, in the ghettos of Soweto and in barrios around the world. He lives on! Forever twenty-five. Forever defiant. Forever hopeful. Forever Tupac.

ONE
Part-Time Mutha

My mother was pregnant with me while she was in prison and a month after she got out of prison she gave birth to me. So I was cultivated in prison; my embryo was in prison.
— TUPAC SHAKUR

Tupac Shakur's mother, Alice Faye Williams, grew up in North Carolina, with her sister Gloria (Glo). When her father Walter Williams, Jr., a truck driver, abruptly moved the family to Norfolk, Virginia, they were propelled into a hellish nightmare. As Alice recalls, "My daddy was a street nigga, and he was loved by the people in the street. He had principles, ethics, and he had a sense of himself. He was a small man, but unafraid. He was stubborn and arrogant." Alice's father had another side to him: He abused her mother behind closed doors. Things finally came to a head when one of his attempted assaults—this time in front of the girls, something her mother did not want her daughters to see—was met with a toss of hot grease straight from the skillet. Alice's mother made a quick relocation to the Bronx, New York, leaving her abuser behind.

"It was hard to hate your parents," Alice says. "It's hard to live with that kind of hatred, because they are a part of you. So in turn, hating them is hating yourself. All that hating hurts. As a girl child, I just hurt. Everything around me seemed hurtful. And, like I said, we had no protection. I never felt safe. Now, I see that I got a lot from my mother. I have learned how to appreciate her strengths and her quiet dignity."

Alice Faye attended New York City's High School of the Performing Arts. She recalls, "A lot of kids that went to PA were coming from private schools. They came to school in limos, and I hated them with a passion. I'd get high off Thunderbird wine before school even started just to deal with my hatred of them. I'd get fucked up with my friends and then go to school and watch them rich kids' limos, pretty clothes, just showing off. This is what my mind was telling me back then, that those kids were showing off. The worst part of the day was lunch because they did not have a cafeteria. No cafeteria. Kids would leave and go to Times Square or Nedick's or the Automat and buy their food. I didn't have money for lunch. My mother begged my bus fare off neighbors just to get me down to the damn place. I was trapped. I could not tell my mother we needed even more money to go to school. So, I'd just leave at lunchtime. Go to school, do my drama and dance classes, and then leave at lunch. I quit or got kicked out. One day I walked into the front door of the school and heard Bobby Kennedy was killed, and I walked out the back door. I figured what the fuck. I had just had it."

After the death of her best friend, Sandra, Alice

was lost. Sandra had a botched hysterectomy, in which the surgeon removed only one tube. She became pregnant without realizing her condition until the fifth month. "So, me and Sandra, we just kept doing our thing: hanging out, doing dope, hittin' the clubs," Alice remembers. "And we tried heroin during this time. This white guy was takin' care of Sandra and he gave it to us. He was white on the outside but he was really black on the inside. He was a street dude and he was good to Sandra.

"Sandra was rushed to the hospital after collapsing on the bathroom floor. She died on the table and the baby lived. The nurses just let the baby die; they chose not to let it live. I was fucked up bad. I walked the streets for a day. She was my best friend and I will miss her . . . forever."

When Alice was around twenty years old she met a man named Shaheed at Manny's Bar on 169th Street in the Bronx, and her life began to change. Shaheed introduced Alice to the lessons of the Nation of Islam and Malcolm X, and even though she never joined the Nation, her search for self began: ". . . as I listened to Brother Shaheed, I began to like me. That's when the chemicals came out of my hair."

Alice's search led her to the Black Power Conference in Philadelphia at Father Paul Washington's Church of the Advocate. It was here that she first saw brothers and sisters in positions of power and authority—an event she says affected her like no other in her life.

In Harlem, around September 1968, at 125th Street and Seventh Avenue, Alice heard Bobby Seale speak at a Black Panther Party rally, and she was hooked.

She says, "It was all over for me then. I heard Bobby Seale recite the Ten Point Program and if you haven't heard that . . . not now when he's an older person, but when he was a young man, he could recite that and recruit a town full of black people just by saying it." Alice had evolved, and she was now and forevermore to be known as Afeni Shakur.

The late 1960s was the height of the Black Panther movement, a movement created by the young Huey P. Newton and led by Bobby Seale to promote a ten-point program of freedom, self-determination of the black and oppressed communities, full employment of black people, the end of the robbery of black and oppressed communities by capitalism, decent housing fit for the shelter of human beings, education that teaches true history and the role of black people in present-day society, free health care for black and oppressed people, an immediate end to police brutality, an immediate end to all wars of aggression, trials by juries of people's peers, and people's community control. The movement caught on in an environment where black people were being disenfranchised and disrespected.

Young Afeni Shakur heard the call and answered, doing whatever she could to help her people. She said to Jasmine Guy in her memoir, *Afeni Shakur: Evolution of a Revolutionary*, "I believed in them.

The principles. The plan. I started the breakfast program to feed children on their way to school. I joined because I could use my mouth for speeches to raise money for the program. I joined 'cause I was fearless. I was a gangster, and I could do whatever was necessary to keep the party alive. I joined for free clinics. I joined for all that because it would have helped my momma if we had that kind of help from our community."

Shortly after Afeni joined the Black Panther Party she became involved with, and then married in a Muslim ceremony, the section leader of Harlem, Lumumba Shakur. As with any other organized group with opposition to the government, the Black Panthers were persecuted. During their brief marriage, Lumumba was arrested in Connecticut. During this time, Afeni rose to a position of power within the party. She flew to the West Coast to meet with Panther founder and leader Huey Newton, to discuss the East and West Coast disputes within the Black Panther Party.

Young Afeni, too, found herself arrested three short months after Lumumba was imprisoned, caught up in a governmental conspiracy charge of blowing up various buildings and landmarks in New York. Afeni had no money and no one to turn to, since her husband was still in jail. With the help of well-meaning white women from various churches, labor movements, and organizations she was able to make bail, not once but twice. While out on bail, Afeni became pregnant by a man she refuses to this day to identify, only saying it is not her then husband Lumumba Shakur.

Afeni was put back in prison after she was granted bail because of the twenty-one defendants she was standing trial with, three fled the country, causing all who were granted bail to forfeit the right. Now in prison and pregnant, Afeni boldly decided to represent herself rather than use one of the Panthers' many lawyers. It has been said that she chose not to accept the female lawyer assigned to her by Lumumba because she feared that the woman's voice was not strong enough to represent her to the fullest.

In the longest trial in New York City history, Afeni Shakur was acquitted of all charges. Newly divorced from Lumumba, Afeni gave birth to a baby boy on June 16, 1971, in Brooklyn, New York. She named him Lesane Parrish Crooks, only to later rename him Tupac Amaru Shakur. Afeni named her son after an Inca Indian revolutionary, Tupac Amaru, meaning "shining serpent." "Shakur" means "Thankful to God" in Arabic.

Afeni's affiliation with the Panther Party made it very difficult for her to find work. She struggled to make ends meet and often moved from house to house and lived sporadically in homeless shelters with her son. For a period of time Afeni and Tupac lived in Harlem. During that time, Tupac met a man who had a profound impact on his view of manhood and perhaps laid the foundation for the movement Tupac later created, T.H.U.G. L.I.F.E. "Legs" was said to be a drug dealer and a street hustler. Tupac later described Legs in an interview: "He didn't even care my moms had a kid. He was like, 'Oh, that's my son.' Took care of me, gave me money, but he was like a criminal, too." It has been said that Legs was arrested for credit card fraud and later died of a crack-induced heart attack. Losing Legs was perhaps one of the most devastating things that happened to Tupac in his young life, as he looked at the man as a father figure.

Afeni never left her Black Panther spirit behind. She secured a job with Legal Services. Afeni's mission remained the same as when she was in the movement, only now she was looking to assist women and children who were left behind by a disintegrating Panther Party. She also had a new man in her life, whom she married. Mutulu Shakur was Afeni's second husband and father to her daughter, Sekyiwa. Mutulu was still involved with the Panther Movement. Once again tragedy struck and Mutulu was arrested and subsequently convicted in 1981 for his involvement in the robbery of an armored truck that left two guards dead. To this day, he is in prison serving a sixty-year sentence.

The rapid decline of the Panther Party saw many of the pivotal figures in Tupac's young life disappearing. Tupac's aunt, Assata Shakur, was convicted of armed robbery, then escaped from jail and fled to Cuba. His godfather, Geronimo Pratt, was sentenced to twenty-five years to life for allegedly killing a schoolteacher. And now Tupac's second father figure had been sent to jail.

Afeni knew that she needed to provide a good role model for her ten-year-old son and sought the counsel and mentorship of the Reverend Herbert Daughtry of the House of the Lord Church in Brooklyn. Daughtry, well known for his social activism, remembered, "I met Afeni years before, as I identified with the Black Panther Party and was close to some of their members, one of which was Afeni. When Afeni decided to join a church she joined our church. Afeni brought her sister Glo, her daughter, and Tupac, who at the time was about eleven."

Through all the tragedy and upheaval in young Tupac's life emerged a talent that Afeni recognized and tried to foster in her son. Afeni enrolled Tupac in a workshop for a Harlem theater group, the 127th Street Ensemble. At the age of twelve, he performed for the first time on the stage of the Apollo Theater in a production of Lorraine Hansberry's *A Raisin in the Sun*. Tupac played the role of Travis, the son of the lead character, Walter Lee Younger. The play details the lives of a family from Chicago with hopes and dreams of escaping urban poverty by moving to the suburbs. Although the role was small, Tupac knew then that he was meant for the stage.

Before Tupac could continue with his newfound love of the theater, his life was uprooted. Seeking a better life and at this point jobless, Afeni moved her family to Baltimore, Maryland. In 1984 Baltimore was known for its high rates of teen pregnancy, black-on-black crime, HIV and AIDS, and poverty.

"We moved to Baltimore, which was a total igno-rance town to me. It gets me upset to talk about it," Tupac said in an interview later, questioning his mother's judgment.

Upon arriving in Baltimore at the age of thirteen, Tupac realized exactly where he was—in the same situation he had just come from, just in a different state. Often Afeni struggled to meet the family's basic needs. Tupac found himself writing and read-ing by candlelight as the family had to forgo power and lights for months at a time.

Tupac was enrolled in Roland Park Middle School, and one year later he entered the Paul Lawrence Dunbar High School. Tupac described as one of his lucky times in Baltimore the opportunity to audition for the Baltimore School for the Arts. He landed a coveted spot at this prestigious institution that prides itself on cultivating the artistic talents of its students.

The Baltimore School for the Arts is housed in an old mansion. Tupac spoke fondly of his experience at the school: "We were exposed to everything. Theater, ballet, different people's lifestyles—rich people's lifestyles, royalty from other countries and things, everything." Tupac developed a lasting friendship with fellow student Jada Pinkett. The two formed a bond that was based on similarities in their shared experiences and the immense talent they both possessed. Tupac wrote his first rap during this time under the name "MC New York." The rhyme's lyrics were inspired by the fatal shooting of a friend.

He also performed in many local talent shows and made a habit of winning.

At this time Tupac found himself at an emerging crossroads in his life. The frustrations of poverty were juxtaposed with the wealth of knowledge and resources he saw every day at school. While living in Baltimore he also found himself gravitating toward community activism, an apparent expansion of his Black Panther roots. He became involved in the Yo-No Campaign, an anti–gun violence campaign headed by community organizer Truxon Sykes; the NAACP; and Baltimore's mayoral race. Tupac's leadership abilities emerged with his involvement with the Young People's Communist League, where he worked with his then girlfriend Mary Baldridge, whose father was the head of the Baltimore Communist Party.

Baltimore had a profound effect on Tupac both personally and professionally. While Tupac was learning how to cultivate his talent at school, he was also battling his and his mother's personal demons at home. His frustrations mounted with his perceived responsibility of being the man of the house. Tupac spent more and more time at the homes of friends. He was becoming accustomed to fending for himself and oftentimes felt he couldn't rely on his mother for his basic needs. Afeni was slowly deteriorating and unable to manage the rearing of a then sixteen-year-old Tupac and ten-year-old Sekyiwa. Sekyiwa was sent to stay with a friend of her mother's, Asante, in Marin City, California, for the summer. Seeing the decline and despair in her situation, Afeni decided to let her daughter remain in California and sent Tupac to be with her while she saved money to join them.

Marin City was poverty stricken, and it soon became apparent to a teenage Tupac exactly where he had ended up. The town had one liquor store, and in the development where he lived, dubbed "The Jungle," the buildings faced multimillion-dollar homes in the city of Tiburon. The homes of the haves, which seemed to mock the abject poverty of the people who lived in The Jungle, served as a constant reminder of what Tupac did not have.

Shortly after Tupac arrived in Marin City, Afeni received a call from her friend Asante and was told that her children, as well as Asante's, would be put in foster care if she didn't come to pick them up. Not equipped to move, Afeni immediately left her job and got on a bus to California. As the bus approached her destination it broke down, and Afeni had to take a cab all the way to Asante's apartment.

Luckily she was able to retrieve Tupac and Sekyiwa from a neighbor, and had to begin the task of starting her life all over again. The abuse and hate to which Asante had exposed the children was heartwrenching. It was especially hard on Tupac, who endured open insults while Asante was in a daily drunken state. Once again Afeni found herself left struggling to put a roof over her family's heads and a way to provide a stable home.

Tupac, then seventeen, could no longer take the uncertainty of his home environment. Where once he was a model student at the Baltimore School for the Arts, now he felt he had to leave school in order to make money to survive. He tried selling drugs, but within a matter of weeks saw that this wasn't going to be his calling. The local dealers told him instead to follow his dream, and in turn they became his sponsors, giving him money here and there to help launch his performing career.

Fueled by the despair that surrounded him in Marin City, Tupac sought out ways to fulfill his desire to perform his music and escape the horrors he saw all around him, including his mother's decline into addiction. During all the tumultuous times of his adolescence he never gave up his love of writing poetry and lyrics. He was also influenced by the desire to create social change. Tupac spoke of wanting to start a Black Panther Party in Marin City to combat the ills of the community. He wanted to start out by teaching pride and respect, just as his mother had taught him, and see where it would go from there.

TWO

Rebel of the Underground

The only thing that comes to a sleeping man is dreams.
— Tupac Shakur

Seeking an outlet for his music, Tupac began attending local shows. It was 1989 and rap music was spreading like wildfire, which only reinforced Tupac's desire to write music and perform. Unfortunately, the rap scene wasn't as progressive in Marin City as elsewhere. Tupac recounted his perspective on the rap scene in Marin City to Davey D in an interview: "Being in Marin City was like a small town so it taught me to be more straightforward with my style. Instead of being so metaphorical with the rhyme, I was encouraged to go straight at it and hit it dead-on and not waste time trying to cover things . . . In Marin City it seemed like things were real country. Everything was straightforward. Poverty was straightforward. There was no way to say 'I'm poor,' but to say 'I'm poor' . . . "

During this time Leila Steinberg, a local Bay Area woman, was organizing a workshop to enable kids to express themselves. Tupac went to a show that Leila organized; he met with her the next day and joined her workshop. Leila recognized his immense talent and wanted to help him nurture it.

Another thing Leila noticed about Tupac was how intelligent he was for his age. "At seventeen he was wide-eyed and thought that he could change the world," she observed. After he had attended the workshop for a few months, it became evident that if Tupac wanted to move further in his career, he needed to be in a more stable environment. Leila invited Tupac and his friend and fellow performer Ray Luv to come live with her, her husband, and their children.

Leila soon realized that she couldn't take Tupac, Ray Luv, and their group, Strictly Dope, to the professional level of their true potential. She called upon a friend in the music industry, Atron Gregory, who was managing a group out of the Bay Area called Digital Underground. Atron had Tupac meet with the group's leader, Shock-G.

Digital Underground was an Oakland-based group that burst on the music scene with originality and funk. The group consisted of Shock-G, Gregory Jacobs, and Chopmaster, and later expanded with Ron Brooks (Money-B) and Earl Cook (Schmoovy-Schmoov). Instead of blending in with the popular rap culture of the time, which included gangsta and political hip-hop, Digital Underground brought a jovial flavor to the rap scene combined with samples of the P-Funk, George Clinton, and Parliament Funkadelic. At the time they already had a single, "Underwater Rhymes," that was put out independently overseas and were finishing their first album, *Sex Packets,* under Tommy Boy Records.

Davey D recalls that a young rap group called the Spice Regime had plans to be the Black Panthers of hip-hop. There was a simultaneous rise of a group on the East Coast with the same vision known as Public Enemy, so, because of that, Digital Underground changed their style and became the funkadelic rap group. The attraction for Tupac went beyond just the music—it was the closeness of the group and the genius of its leader, Shock-G.

Shock-G described his first meeting with Tupac as intense. Tupac was eager to impress him and put his all into the meeting. Shock-G saw the promise in Tupac and told Atron so. Shock-G had many things in common with Tupac besides talent and a love of music. He had spent a lot of his childhood moving from place to place along the East Coast before settling in the Bay Area. He, too, had dropped out of high school and became involved in a life of crime before deciding to attend college and study music.

Tupac's group Strictly Dope broke up in 1989. Even though the group was signed to Atron's label, TNT Records, things weren't progressing fast enough. Atron decided to try to keep Tupac despite the breakup of Strictly Dope, inviting him to go on tour with Digital Underground. Tupac was then scheduled to travel with Digital Underground as a roadie and backup dancer. Unsure whether this was his best opportunity, he sought the advice of his older stepbrother, Mopreme, who was also out in

Oakland. Mopreme had already had a hit rhyming on Tony Toni Tone's *Feels Good* under the name Mosecedes. Tupac asked him if he should go on tour with Digital Underground, because he was torn and ready to go to Atlanta in search of new opportunities. Mopreme encouraged Tupac to go on tour.

Tupac wasn't just a roadie. As Money-B recalls, "He came to assist us with anything we needed to happen. He would sometimes carry whatever he had to carry, but he was part of the stage show. We made sure we allowed him a part of the show to rhyme. He had parts in the show. He'd do the Humpty Dance; he would also dance when he needed to dance, him and I."

While touring with Digital Underground, Tupac met many other artists on the tour, including Big Daddy Kane and his then manager, Jeffrey Calendar. Tupac was a big fan of Kane, who was headlining the tour. He loved Kane's rap style and offered to help carry in his equipment. Kane and his crew instantly liked Tupac.

The debut release of the album *Sex Packets* with the hit single "Doowutchyalike" garnered great reviews, and within months the single was certified platinum. The album had other wildly successful tracks such as "The Humpty Dance," an anthem of the group's alter ego, Humpty Hump. "The Humpty Dance" climbed to the top of both the pop and the R&B charts. The website YBfree.com states that "Digital Underground's declaration and the funky dance took rap to a new level; allowing people to, like the rap group itself, not take itself seriously and just have a good time. Humpty Hump cemented the group's place in hip-hop lure, but Tupac would keep them there forever."

Although Tupac fully became a part of the Digital Underground, he still maintained his outspoken personality. Tupac earned the name "Rebel of the Underground" for his candid manner and up-front way of dealing with life: " . . . I'm more the rebel (of the group). I speak for the young black males. I feel as though I can honestly say my ear is to the streets. Especially for the young black males in America in the ghettos, my ear is right there." Money-B and Tupac also had a lot in common. They were the closest group members in age, and both liked to party. One of the more critical links was that both Money-B's father and Tupac's mother were Black Panthers. Money-B understood the fight in Tupac and the rebel mentality.

The other side of Tupac that came to show itself to the group was his need for perfection. Tupac was a perfectionist on tour. He was also known for trying to upstage fellow band members because he thought they weren't doing justice to the song. His need for control caused many fights among the group. Shock-G stated in an interview, "Do you know how many times I fired Pac?! . . . It would be livid . . . almost fighting. Then two hours later knock, knock, 'Yo what's up? Come on, let's go get some hos.' All right."

The Digital Underground members adopted Tupac as part of the family, filling the void of the family he left behind in Marin City while on the road. Atron and others have described this time as one of the happiest and carefree times in Tupac's life. "I look back with the greatest fondness. Those were like some of the best times in my life. It's all funny to me, it's all good," Tupac said of his times with Digital Underground.

While on tour, Tupac worked on his own music with the help of Shock-G. Things were going well despite some incidents that caused Tupac to clash with others on the tour, such as an occurrence while on tour in Augusta, Georgia. The soundman for the whole tour did something that the group wasn't happy with, and Tupac couldn't take it. He went to punch the soundman, but Atron stepped in and grabbed him, which prevented the shutdown of the whole tour. "Whenever there was a battle Tupac was right there. Any chance he could get to get on the mic he was there," said Money-B.

Because of his drive and talent, Shock-G gave Tupac more opportunities to perform and a featured spot on Digital Underground's second album, *This Is an E.P. Release.* There was no going back from there, so when the group was asked to do a song for the soundtrack for Dan Aykroyd's new film *Nothing But Trouble,* Shock-G gave Tupac another chance to shine. Tupac was not only featured on the hit single "Same Song," but also had a cameo with the group in the movie.

With all these amazing things happening to Tupac, the news while on tour of his mother's addiction to crack came as a blow. Tupac loved his mother dearly despite her addiction. She was his hero, but he knew there was nothing he could do to help her. It may seem a little ironic because Tupac had been known among his band mates to always smoke weed and drink. In an interview Tupac regarded weed as harmless and said he was always drunk and high off of weed when he recorded his music because he felt the people who listened to his music were drunk or high when they listened to it. He remained on tour and began to plan for his first solo album, *2Pacalypse Now*, for TNT Records. Tupac was also working on a movie that was scheduled to be released a few months after his album came out. He was finally living his dream.

THREE
I Get Around

*I am real. The lyrics might be a story or they might be real.
But I stay real, I am never a story, never a script, never a character.*

— TUPAC SHAKUR

While back in Oakland awaiting the release of *2Pacalypse Now*, Tupac seemed to have everything that he'd dreamed of since his days in Baltimore. He was a member of a successful rap group, his first solo album was going to be released in less than a month, and he finally wasn't feeling the vice grip of poverty. With all this good fortune, an unsuspecting Tupac was crossing a street in Oakland on his way to the bank when he was stopped by two police officers for jaywalking.

According to the claim he filed for damages, Tupac stated that he was physically and verbally assaulted as well as falsely arrested and imprisoned by two white Oakland police officers. In his complaint, Tupac said that after he asked for his ticket using a profanity, the officers put him in a chokehold until he lost consciousness despite his never assaulting or resisting the officers. Tupac claimed he was facedown in a gutter when he regained consciousness, and that the officers told him that he was going to learn his place while in Oakland. Being assaulted by the police was exactly what Tupac had heard about from his mother when she spoke to him at a very young age about the brutality she and the other Black Panthers had to endure. Tupac himself talked about the injustice of police brutality on many occasions, and now he himself was the victim. He observed, "I had no record all my life . . . No police record until I made a record. As my video was debuting on MTV, I was behind bars getting beat up by the police department. I was still an N-I-Double-G-A and they proved it."

Tupac became a local celebrity when *2Pacalypse Now* was released. Everyone in Oakland knew who he was, and on the same day his lawyer filed a $10 million lawsuit for damages against the Oakland Police Department, making the release of his first solo album bittersweet.

2Pacalypse Now didn't take off the way Tupac had hoped. There were problems marketing the album because it wasn't like the material he had recorded with Digital Underground. It wasn't that head-bopping, musically lyrical, makes-you-want-to-dance music. Like the outspoken Tupac, *2Pacalypse Now* graphically addressed social issues of young black males that included, ironically, police brutality. It also addressed ghetto themes of poverty, teenage pregnancy, and drug use, all of which he'd seen growing up. That's where Interscope Records came in. Atron was making a deal with Interscope. Tom Whalley, the company's president, brought in one of Tupac's demos for Ted Field's verdict. Ted gave the demo to his daughter; she loved it and told her dad that they had to sign this artist. Upon the advice of his daughter, Ted and Tom signed Tupac to Interscope on August 15. Interscope signed a deal with TNT, which had TNT furnish Interscope with an undisclosed number of Tupac albums in exchange for certain unspecified advances and royalties from Interscope.

Tupac wasn't awarded the $10 million claim against the Oakland Police Department; instead, he walked away with approximately $42,000. More important, the principle of the Oakland Police Department having to pay a black man something for their acts of hatred spurred him on.

In January of 1992, Tupac's first movie, Ernest Dickerson's *Juice,* was released. When Money-B went to audition for the part of Bishop, their road manager suggested Tupac go along with Money-B to see if he could get a part in the movie too. Tupac auditioned and immediately embodied the role of Bishop. He won the part over a friend, East Coast rapper Treach from Naughty by Nature, who was also auditioning for the role. Tupac sealed the deal by getting so into the part that he threw a chair across the room. Even Treach thought that Tupac was so good he deserved the part.

Tupac received great reviews for his performance. In an interview with Davey D, he talked about the movie: "The movie is about four kids and their coming of age. It's not a hip-hop movie. It's a real good movie that happens to have hip-hop in it. If it was made in the '60s it would've depicted whatever was 'down' in the '60s . . . My character is Roland Bishop, a psychotic, insecure, very violent, very short-tempered individual." The movie brought attention to Tupac as an actor, but his album was being noticed, too.

Just when things were starting to get back on track after his run-in with the Oakland Police, Tupac gained national notoriety in a way he'd never intended. On April 11, 1992, five short months after *2Pacalypse Now* was released, eighteen-year-old Ronald Ray Howard was arrested for the shooting of Department of Public Safety trooper Bill Davidson in Jackson County, Texas, after a high-speed chase in a stolen vehicle.

Ronald Howard had had previous run-ins with the law, with charges including "unauthorized use of a motor vehicle." At the time of the shooting, Howard claimed that he was influenced by Tupac's music and in particular the song "Sister Souljah," which depicts the shooting of a cop who pulls someone over after a car chase. A jury eventually found Howard guilty. They gave no credence to his defense that rap music, in particular Tupac's music, made him commit the murder. The Texas state judge said that the music shouldn't be blamed for the shooting, but noted there was content in the album relating to killing cops. The State was going to try to ban Tupac's music in Texas. In exchange for keeping his music in stores, Tupac agreed to never perform in Texas again. But that didn't stop the trooper's widow from filing a multimillion-dollar civil suit against Tupac, Interscope, and Time Warner. After thirteen years on Texas's death row, Ronald Howard was put to death by the State of Texas on October 6, 2005. But it was too late; the damage was already done to further tarnish and demonize Tupac.

Everything was happening so fast for Tupac—both the good and the bad—that it had become hard to keep up with the frenetic pace of his life. He was being pulled in many directions, and money, fame, and notoriety were taking over. The year 1992 was proving to be a pivotal one in Tupac's emerging career.

In May, Tupac had a chance encounter with Interscope labelmate Marion "Suge" Knight. Suge (short for Sugar Bear), co-founder of Death Row Records, had his own backstory in the music industry. A former University of Nevada football player, who played for the Los Angeles Rams for a short time, he turned his attention to the music industry in 1989, founding his own music publishing company. It was rumored that Suge made a name for himself in the industry by forcing Vanilla Ice, a white rapper from Florida, to sign over his publishing royalties from his multiplatinum album *To the Extreme*. Suge said that Ice had sampled from one of his company's creations. Robert Van Winkle, a.k.a. Vanilla Ice, said, "He took me over to the balcony, and he had me look over. He says to me, 'You're gonna sign these papers' . . . I signed it. I gave millions away." Later Ice recanted his story, refusing to talk about it publicly again.

Having been in the industry for a few years, Suge

decided to form an artist management company. He signed many rappers well known to the West Coast, including DJ Quick and D.O.C. Suge also met Dr. Dre, who, at the time, was in royalty disputes with Eazy-E and Ruthless Records. Dr. Dre no longer wanted to be a part of NWA (Niggaz With Attitude) after producing the NWA album *Niggaz4life* in 1991. The album landed at number one on the *Billboard* album chart, but Dr. Dre was unhappy because he felt that Eazy-E was keeping most of the profits. That same year, Suge managed to negotiate a deal releasing Dr. Dre from his Ruthless Records contract. Eazy-E and manager Jerry Heller tell a similar story to Vanilla Ice's of intimidation and threats with pipes and baseball bats by Suge's boys. In 1991, Suge and Dr. Dre co-founded Death Row Records. Suge said he wanted Death Row to be the Motown of the '90s, so it's no wonder why he would want to sign a talent like Tupac.

Unfortunately it was becoming evident very fast that Suge was going to run Death Row the way he was rumored to get his artists. During the recording of the multiplatinum Death Row debut album *The Chronic,* aspiring rappers George and Lynwood Stanley claimed Suge pistol-whipped them and ordered them to remove their clothes, because one of the brothers used a phone without Suge's permission. The allegations got Suge arrested; he received seven years' probation and later settled out of court for civil damages with the brothers. Combined with his prior criminal record and rumored strong-arm tactics, Suge was building a reputation for himself and Death Row that would later collide with Tupac's own drama-filled life.

Yet until that time, Tupac regarded Suge with respect. Tupac said, "I used to always see Suge. When they did the soundtrack for *Murder Was the Case* and I was going through all those legal problems he was like, 'Yo, give me a song, dog.' I gave him a song and I got the most I ever got for a song. It was damn near an album budget. I got something like $200,000 for one song and they didn't even use it, but I still got paid for everything I did for the soundtrack. He had asked me to come to Death Row and I told him I wasn't ready. Instead of taking it personal he did that for me and I appreciated that."

Tupac also stayed focused on his personal mission of uplifting his people. He created a movement based on a code of ethics for the streets that he called T.H.U.G. L.I.F.E. He even got T.H.U.G. L.I.F.E. tattooed across his stomach at a local tattoo parlor in Los Angeles. T.H.U.G. L.I.F.E. was more to Tupac than just a tattoo; it was a code of honor. Tupac said, "I didn't create T.H.U.G. L.I.F.E., I diagnosed it." He wrote this code with the help of his stepfather, Mutulu Shakur, and others. T.H.U.G. L.I.F.E. was an acronym for The Hate U Gave Lil' Infants Fucks Everyone.

In an interview, Erica Ford spoke fondly of Tupac:

> *I first met Tupac at his lawyer, Michael Warren's, home. What struck me about him was his soul; what he was made of, his realness. He*

had a deep desire to not lose his roots in terms of where he came from and being able to take that sense of self into the music industry through his music. Tupac felt he related to the young people, and that thug element—which no one wanted to relate to—he related to the most.

I had been working in the struggle since the age of nineteen with Tupac's stepfather Mutulu Shakur, Viola Plummer, and Michael Warren. I was involved with the December 12 movement and the political movements in and around New York City. I worked with Chaz Williams of Black Hand Entertainment and made The Code.

Mutulu Shakur wrote a letter to me and sent a copy of The Code and asked that I give The Code to Tupac. The Code gave a charge to those brothers in organizing their constituents. The same day I went to the Meridian Hotel to hand deliver The Code to Tupac; ironically that very night the incident with the young woman [Ayanna Jackson, who accused Tupac of sexual abuse in November 1993] occurred. I believe the government knew that Tupac would make this a reality. I don't think that the counterintelligence program to destroy the Panthers ever stopped. They may have not thought that Tupac was any different than Huey P. Newton, who was able to galvanize the young people in his day. Tupac had star power, he had the resources for economic development, and he had the ability to mobilize young people to take over their communities in a positive way.

The Code of T.H.U.G. L.I.F.E.

1. All new Jacks to the game must know: a) He's going to get rich. b) He's going to jail. c) He's going to die.
2. Crew Leaders: You are responsible for legal/financial payment commitments to crew members; your word must be your bond.
3. One crew's rat is every crew's rat. Rats are now like a disease; sooner or later we all get it; and they should too.
4. Crew leader and posse should select a diplomat, and should work ways to settle disputes. In unity, there is strength!
5. Carjacking in our Hood is against the Code.
6. Slinging to children is against the Code.
7. Having children slinging is against the Code.
8. No slinging in schools.
9. Since the rat Nicky Barnes opened his mouth, ratting has become accepted by some. We're not having it.
10. Snitches is outta here.
11. The Boys in Blue don't run nothing; we do. Control the Hood, and make it safe for squares.
12. No slinging to pregnant Sisters. That's baby killing; that's genocide!
13. Know your target, who's the real enemy.
14. Civilians are not a target and should be spared.
15. Harm to children will not be forgiven.
16. Attacking someone's home where their family is

known to reside must be altered or checked.

17. Senseless brutality and rape must stop.
18. Our old folks must not be abused.
19. Respect our Sisters. Respect our Brothers.
20. Sisters in the Life must be respected if they respect themselves.
21. Military disputes concerning business areas within the community must be handled professionally and not on the block.
22. No shooting at parties.
23. Concerts and parties are neutral territories; no shooting!
24. Know the Code; it's for everyone.
25. Be a real ruff neck. Be down with the Code of the Thug Life.
26. Protect yourself at all times.

Tupac and a group of community leaders and I met with some of the OG's (Original Gangsters) in Manhattan, Brooklyn, and Queens. There was discussion around the necessity to be able to see the bigger picture, a need to change how we as a people related to the community and see the importance of educating the young people to be the lawyers, accountants, the marketing people we needed as a community to exist. We also discussed the need to protect the community, especially our seniors. Tupac spoke out on economic development; he sold 1 million records and his philosophy was if he collected just $1 from those 1 million people we could help begin to build schools and institutions. The sad thing is of the Original Gangsters from Queens we met with, about four of them subsequently were killed, arrested, or incarcerated.

The Code movement was organized, Tupac made sure that the Outlawz were well read and knowledgable, they had community control. His philosophy was that we did not have to remain oppressed. We have the power within ourselves collectively.

We did a concert out of Wilkins Park on June 18, 1994, to launch The Code. Footage of that event can be seen in the movie Resurrection. Performing that day was Tupac, Fat Joe, Naughty By Nature, Dead Presidents, and others. The Code foundation built and developed leaders and developed a code of conduct in the street, it deals with gang violence and the rise of crime in our communities. The event was attended by 5,000 people including OG's and some of the younger people and it was peaceful. They embraced The Code because he was Tupac. After that people wanted to get down with it and spread it. A peace campaign between Jamaica, Queens' 40 Housing Projects, and Baisley Housing Projects was established. The senseless murders were significantly reduced for a period of time and it made an impact and transformed lives.

Tupac was making a name for himself in both the music and movie world. John Singleton, who had just made his directorial and writing debut with the critically acclaimed movie *Boyz n the Hood,* chose Tupac to play the love interest opposite Janet Jackson in his new film, *Poetic Justice.* Tupac was grateful for the part because it gave him the opportunity to disprove the rumors that he had just gotten lucky with the role of Bishop in *Juice* because he was playing himself rather than acting.

The filming of *Poetic Justice* took place in South Central Los Angeles, but paused during the 1992 L.A. riots. The riots began on April 29, when a mostly white jury acquitted four police officers accused in the videotaped beating of black motorist Rodney King. Thousands of enraged people, mostly young black and Latino males, took to the streets of Los Angeles burning, looting, and fighting anyone in their way. In a video interview, Tupac said he had joined them. Fifty to sixty people were killed during the riots, and even victim Rodney King pleaded for peace, asking, "Can we get along here? Can we all just get along?"

There was also dissension on the set of the film. Tupac said, "I don't know if it was Janet that it came from, but I know that they suddenly, out of the blue, wanted me to take an AIDS test for this love scene and I did not agree. I did not disagree if we were going to make love. I said, 'If I could make love to Janet Jackson I'd take four AIDS tests, but, if I'm going to do a love scene with her just like somebody else did, and they didn't take a test, I'm not taking a test."

DMaq and Tupac recorded *Strictly 4 My Niggaz* on the first day of the Los Angeles riots after the beating of Rodney King. The rapper Tone Loc and his posse, the West Side Tribe, were personal friends of DMaq. Tupac said, "We played basketball and hung out. Tone introduced me to Lay Law, one of the original members of NWA, and we have been friends ever since and producing partners. We were independent producers and worked for who we wanted."

DMaq recalls, "Lay Law called me one day and asked if I wanted to work with Tupac and I said, hell yeah. This was in 1991 and I went to New York City for a Sony development deal around that same time. When I came back from New York I was introduced to Ice Cube and Tupac. He was real. Just a cool down-to-earth dude. We recorded 'Heaven's Got a Ghetto' on my four-track in my home studio first in 1991 and we rerecorded 'Heaven's Got a Ghetto' and it was released a few years later.

"Right there as the drama unfolded I watched as Tupac became emotionally charged. He rewrote the lyrics and we laid the track down in no time. He took out his anger on the microphone. After the session we all disbursed. That night was emotional and it reflected what he was going through that night."

It was proving to be a long, hot summer for Tupac in 1992, and it was about to get a little hotter. The many incidents in 1992 began when Tupac was charged with battery for slapping a woman who asked for his autograph. Then on August 22, Tupac was invited to perform at a festival celebrating the fiftieth anniversary of Marin City. Tupac arrived in his brand-new Jeep ready to perform. While he was signing autographs, a fight broke out. Tupac was punched in the face by a Marin City resident over something negative he had said about the city. Tupac had a .380 Colt automatic that was registered to him in his backpack. He yelled to his stepbrother Mopreme to get the gun. Several shots were fired, and one killed a child in the crowd, Qu'id Walker Teal. The crowd got ugly and began to chase Tupac, who jumped over a fence and got into his car. He drove down the street and got out of the car. The crowd followed him, totally wrecking the car with bats, bottles, and bricks. They were pelting Tupac with rocks, so he hid under a police car until police calmed the crowd down. Then he was taken to the substation in Sausalito, where he and Mopreme were arrested. The police held Tupac for twelve hours, but no one was charged with the shooting due to lack of evidence. Detectives later found a spent .380-caliber shell casing, a gun in the bushes, and .380-caliber ammunition in the Jeep. Tupac's second wrongful death suit was about to be filed against him, for the death of little Qu'id.

The connection of *2Pacalypse Now* with the earlier shooting of the state trooper in Texas, coupled with the latest string of events in Tupac's life, generated great media attention. In September, Vice President Dan Quayle publicly criticized Tupac's lyrics and made a direct connection between Ronald Howard's actions and Tupac's music. Quayle made the statement, "There's no reason for a record like this to be released. It has no place in our society," provoking journalist Marcus Leshock to ask, "Was it really the record that Dan Quayle thought had no place in our society, or was it Tupac?"

Tupac was amazed that someone in a high governmental position would even take notice of him, a kid from the ghetto. It was then that the public began to see the emergence of the true rebel that Tupac was about to become—the rebel born out of a movement, the rebel that a mother reared to speak his mind, the rebel that they made their worst nightmare.

Despite all the controversy, Tupac was still in high demand. He was looking forward to his second solo album, to be released in five months. Tupac was working on this album with people who knew him personally and professionally and hoped old friends like Shock-G could give him some songs with mass appeal. He was looking for this album to trump his first. Knowing Tupac gave this group of producers an advantage; they knew the Tupac before all the controversy. The guy that just wanted to smoke weed, drink, and bag hos. They also knew the political side of Tupac, the enlightened lyricist who drew his lyrics from a higher place. That's where songs like "I Get Around," "Keep Ya Head Up," and "Holler if You Hear Me" came from.

Watching MTV, Tupac found out that Allen and Albert Hughes had dropped him from the video for "Menace II Society." Tupac said, "They was doin' all my videos. After I did *Juice,* they said, 'Can we use your name to get this movie deal?' I said, 'Hell yeah.'" Tupac was originally attached as the lead, but was fired after a fight with director Allen Hughes.

Strictly 4 My Niggaz was released on February 1, 1993, and it looked like things were improving for Tupac. It was a new year, and Tupac had every hope that this year would be better than the tumultuous year that had just ended. He had a new album out, a movie coming out, and he was going to work on collaborations with his half brother Mopreme and his boys on his brainchild, *Thug Life Volume I.* Everything was sweet for Tupac. Or was it?

March 13 proved to be the beginning of a public decline for Tupac. After making a guest appearance on the popular Keenan Ivory Wayans television show *In Living Color,* Tupac and his boys got in the limo waiting for them in the studio parking lot. Tupac, in his usual fashion, was getting ready to smoke a blunt. The limo driver, David DeLeon, complained to Tupac and his boys that he didn't want drugs in his car. DeLeon claimed that they then got out of the car and beat him up. Police found marijuana and a gun on Tupac, and he was arrested but wasn't charged. He was released on $15,000 bail. Later, DeLeon filed a civil suit against Tupac that was settled in June of 1996 for an undisclosed sum of money.

Less than a month later, Tupac's famous temper flared up at a Lansing, Michigan, concert. On April 5, while performing onstage, Tupac swung at a local rapper with a baseball bat. He was sentenced to ten days in jail for this incident. Things were getting out of control, and Tupac's friends and family members were becoming concerned. His erratic behavior was widely publicized. It seemed that every time you turned on a television or opened a newspaper, there would be Tupac in another incident. Some wondered if he could hold it together for the premiere of *Poetic Justice*.

Fortunately, Tupac made it to June without adding any new incidents to the laundry list of events from the past twelve months. He even appeared on the television show *A Different World* with his old friend from Baltimore, Jada Pinkett. Tupac played her boyfriend Picolo on the show, giving a realistic portrayal of a young black man in love with the girl who left him to go off to college. It was as though Jada and Tupac were actually playing out their own story.

Poetic Justice was released on July 23, 1993, to mixed reviews. Tupac's performance revealed a different side of the actor than he'd shown in *Juice*. Desson Howe of the *Washington Post* wrote, "Shakur is wonderful too, with an immensely appealing, laid-back sexiness." The laid-back Tupac is the Tupac that friends and family talk of when remembering his youth. It is the Tupac seen in an interview videotaped when he was seventeen: an articulate, contemplative young man with so many thoughts on changing the world. While the public was seeing glimpses of that side of Tupac, at the time they were mainly caught up in the negativity surrounding him.

While Tupac's prior indiscretions connected him with drugs, guns, and the wrongful death of an innocent child, he was about to blow up in the public eye in a way that would begin to shape his downfall. On October 31, Tupac went to Clark Atlanta University to do a concert. It was reported by some media outlets that after the concert at Clark, Tupac and his friends almost hit Mark and Scott Whitwell, brothers and suburban police officers, who were off-duty, walking in plainclothes with Mark's wife at the Piedmont and Springs intersection. Tupac maintained that he saw the Whitwells harassing a black man in a traffic dispute. Tupac said he got out of his car and asked what was going on and as he did this, the man drove off. It's unclear what happened next, but by witness accounts, Mark pulled out a gun and fired first. Tupac then leaned over the roof of his car and released three shots, which hit Mark in the abdomen and Scott in the buttocks.

Tupac was arrested and charged with two counts of aggravated assault and released on bail. During the hearing, many fascinating details came out about the incident. The investigating detective admitted the officers' report stated that "niggers came by and did a drive-by shooting." It was also discovered that the Whitwells had been drinking, and the prosecution's witness testified that the gun fired at Tupac had been seized in a drug bust and then stolen from an evidence locker. Eventually the charges against Tupac were dropped.

The altercation with the Atlanta officers would

prove to be another pivotal moment in Tupac's career. It fueled his ego and, to his mind, proved his philosophy of the police department's all-out onslaught on black men. It also encouraged an already paranoid Tupac to be skeptical of those around him. Ironically, Tupac's song "I Get Around" was topping the R&B charts during this tumultuous time, which was going to become even more tumultuous in a matter of weeks.

FOUR
Keep Ya Head Up

Being famous and having money gave me confidence. The screams of the crowd gave me confidence. Before that I was a shell of a man.

—TUPAC SHAKUR

Tupac's astrological sign—Gemini, the sign of the twins—proved to be an ongoing theme in his life. When things were going well for Tupac, there was a flip side to that good fortune. Tupac was in New York filming his third major motion picture, *Above the Rim,* for Jeff Pollack and New Line Cinema. Tupac played the role of Birdie, a charismatic drug-dealing street hustler. As with his other roles, Tupac tried to fully embody his character onscreen.

On the set of *Above the Rim*, Tupac met a man named Nigel, also known as Haitian Jack and Jacques Agnant. Nigel introduced him to his friend Trevor, and both were alleged members of the "Black Mafia," a syndicate of drug dealers out of New York. Nigel was the perfect subject for Tupac to study for the part of Birdie; he was Birdie personified.

Nigel and Trevor took Tupac out and showed him a good time in New York, introducing him to William "King Tut" Johnson, who was the head of the Black Mafia. According to Tupac, "I used to dress in baggies and sneakers. They took me shopping, that's when I bought my Rolex and all my jewels. They made me mature. They introduced me to all these gangsters in Brooklyn. I met Nigel's family, went to his kid's birthday party. I trusted him. I even tried to get Nigel in the movie, but he didn't want to be on film. That bothered me. I don't know any nigga that didn't want to be in the movies." Nigel and Trevor wanted Tupac to join the BadBoy Records label, but Tupac refused.

It was a clear and brisk Sunday night; the date was November 14, 1993. Nigel and Trevor picked Tupac up and took him to a club on 14th Street called Nell's. Formerly an old electronics warehouse, Nell's was the place to go on a Sunday night for a laid-back good time. This is where accounts of the evening divide. Tupac said, "Nigel and Trevor took me to Nell's. I was meeting Ronnie Lott from the New York Jets and Derrick Coleman from the Nets."

Tupac was introduced to a young woman by the name of Ayanna Jackson, who was said to be Nigel's friend. "Money came to me and said, 'This girl wants to do more than meet you.' I already knew what that meant. She wanted to fuck. I just left them and went to the dance floor by myself. Then this girl came out and started dancing. So I'm dancing to this reggae music, she's touching my dick, she's touching my balls, she opened my zipper, she put her hands on me. There's a little dark part in Nell's, and I see people over there making out already, so she starts pushing me this way. We go over in the corner. She pulled my dick out; she started sucking my dick on the dance floor. Soon as she finished that—just enough to get me solid, rock-hard—we got off the dance floor. I told Nigel, 'I've got to get out of here. I'm about to take her to the hotel.' Nigel was, like, 'No, no, no. I'm going to take you back.' We drive to the hotel. We go upstairs and have sex, real quick. As soon as I came, that was it. She left me her number, and everything was cool. Nigel was spending the night in my room all these nights. When he found out she sucked my dick on the floor and we had sex, he and Trevor were livid!"

By all accounts, four days later, on November 18, Ayanna's and Tupac's paths would cross again. According to Tupac, "We had a show to do in New Jersey at Club 88. We went shopping, we got dressed up, we were all ready. Nigel was saying, 'Why don't you give her a call?' So we were all sitting in the hotel, drinking. I'm waiting for the show, and Nigel's like, 'I called her. I mean, she called me, and she's on her way.' We were watching TV when the phone rings, and she's downstairs. She came upstairs looking all nice, dressed all provocative and shit. So we're all sitting there talking, and she's making me uncomfortable, because instead of sitting with Nigel and them, she's sitting on the arm of my chair. So we get in the room, I'm laying on my stomach, she's massaging my back. I turn around. She starts massaging my front. This lasted for about a half an hour. I'm thinking she's about to give me another blow job, but before she could do that, some niggas came in, and I froze up more than she froze up. So they came and they started touching her ass. I just got up and walked out of the room. When I went to the other suite, Man Man told me that Talibah, my publicist at the time, had been there for a while and was waiting in the bedroom of that suite. I went to see Talibah and we talked about what she had been doing during the day, then I went and laid down on the couch and went to sleep. When I woke up, Nigel was standing over me going, 'Pac, Pac,' and all the lights was on in both rooms. I didn't know how much time had passed. So when I woke up, it was, like, 'You're going to the police, you're going to the police.' Nigel walks out of the room, comes back with the girl. She's not making sense. 'I came to see you. You let them do this to me.' I'm, like, 'I don't got time for this shit right here.' She said, 'This not the last time you're going to hear from me,' and slammed the door. And Nigel goes, 'Don't worry about it, Pac, don't worry.' I asked him what happened, and he was, like, 'Too many niggas.' Niggas start going downstairs, but nobody was coming back upstairs."

Tupac, his road manager, Man Man, also known as Charles Fuller, and Nigel were arrested after Ayanna Jackson reported the incident to hotel security, who then called the police. Ms. Jackson said that Man Man never touched her, and an unidentified friend of Nigel's was the third person who raped her. The friend left the hotel before the police arrived and has never been identified or prosecuted. In the hotel suites, police found a twenty-minute videotape that showed Tupac and a woman (not Ms. Jackson) engaged in a sex act and two guns belonging to Tupac and Man Man. On November 20, Tupac was freed on bond after posting $50,000 bail.

At the hearing, Paul Brenner, attorney for Jacques Agnant (a.k.a. Nigel), requested that his client's case be severed from Tupac Shakur and Charles Fuller's case because they were facing a weapons charge and his client was not. The prosecutor didn't oppose the severing of the cases, and the judge granted the request. Indictments for sexual abuse and sodomy were handed down to Tupac Shakur, Charles Fuller, and Jacques Agnant.

In December, John Singleton was forced by Columbia Pictures to drop Tupac as Malik, the lead in his new movie, *Higher Learning,* because of his arrests. In an article written by Kevin Powell in *VIBE* magazine, Singleton was quoted as saying, "Basically, since all this stuff is happening, the media is trying to play 'good nigga vs. bad nigga' and say I don't want him in the movie. That ain't true. In their minds, it doesn't matter if he's guilty or not. They don't want nothin' to do with him. I talked to Tupac and said, 'I still got your back.' "

Tupac's face was everywhere, and not just because of the rape charge. He was doing so much work both prior to and after the charge was made that he was hard to miss. During this time, Tupac needed to be surrounded by friends and family as much as possible. He reconnected with his dear friend Jada and attended the premiere of her new movie, *A Low Down Dirty Shame,* with her, and he appeared in Salt-N-Pepa's "Whatta Man" video with his good friend Treach.

Of course, there's no way to avoid the negative publicity when you are a major public figure charged with rape. Tupac did his best, but the anger at his betrayal by people that he'd believed in and trusted bubbled over. March 10, 1994, two short weeks before the release of *Above the Rim,* Tupac ran into Allen and Albert Hughes on the set of a Spice 1 video they were directing. Because of their prior beef surrounding a role Tupac was supposed to play in *Menace II Society* and their dropping him from the film without telling him, there was a lot of bad blood between Tupac and the brothers. Tupac went up to Allen and hit him while his brother Albert ran off. Allen said Tupac came at him with a bunch of his boys at his side. Tupac said, "The niggas knew them just like they knew me, from around the way. I got them niggas started making videos anyway. Plus, I came ready to kick both they asses myself. Those other niggas didn't get with T.H.U.G. L.I.F.E. until after that shit happened." Tupac was arrested and charged with assault and battery and for carrying a loaded, concealed gun. He even bragged about the incident on *Yo! MTV Raps* to host Ed Lover. Tupac was later sentenced to fifteen days in jail, and subsequently Allen Hughes filed a civil suit against him.

Trouble was finding Tupac everywhere he went.

He was becoming the poster child for the ills of America, and the media was there to point the finger every time. On a clear Friday night, Tupac and a friend were speeding down Hollywood Boulevard. They were pulled over by the police, who found marijuana and a loaded 9-millimeter semiautomatic in the car. Tupac was arrested and released the next day on $1,000 bail.

Tupac's vision for T.H.U.G. L.I.F.E. was about to emerge full force. *Above the Rim* was released, and Tupac's performance was called convincing by Roger Ebert. Desson Howe of the *Washington Post* said, "Shakur, who saunters and slithers his way through every scene he's in, is undeniably watchable. With his hypnotic, sleepy-eyed expression, he suggests a scheming lynx on Quaaludes." After recording the album *Thug Life: Thug Life Vol. 1* during all the drama in the fall of 1993, its first single, "Pour Out a Little Liquor," was released on the *Above the Rim* sound track. The group Thug Life featured Tupac, Big Syke, Macadoshis, Mopreme, and The Rated R.

Tupac was still in high demand. He was recording a new album, doing concerts and appearances, and trying to keep his head up through this trying time. Kevin Powell reported his words and demeanor for *VIBE* magazine.

"Some days I wake up and it wouldn't take nothin' for me to go, 'POW!' " He points an imaginary gun at his head. "But I wouldn't do that because I don't want no one to think that's the

way to go." Tupac stares across his barely furnished living room. He reaches for his pack of cigarettes, lights one, then sucks in hard.

"It was all right with the police thing [in Atlanta], but this rape shit . . . " He draws in a deep breath. "It kills me." A pause. " 'Cuz it ain't me." His voice rises and he grows visibly angry. "What was all that 'Keep Ya Head Up,' 'Brenda's Got a Baby'? What was all that for? To just be charged with rape?" He seems close to tears.

"I love black women," he continues. "It has made me love them more because there are black women who ain't trippin' off this. But it's made me feel real about what I said in the beginning: There are sisters and there's bitches."

While Tupac had a reputation for being seen with a lot of beautiful women, there was no one woman in his life. Having a fast-paced life never seemed suitable for having a steady girlfriend. Yet when Tupac met nineteen-year-old Keisha Morris, that all changed. Keisha was an unassuming girl who wasn't a part of the music industry. She was a petite, sweet girl who was going to school and working. Tupac described her as "a good girl . . . a real square." Perhaps that was her appeal for him. She wasn't like other women, who just wanted to say they'd slept with him. After a chance second meeting, Tupac began to pursue Keisha and to acknowledge her as his girlfriend.

In September, at Milwaukee's MECCA Arena, Tupac's uncanny magnetism for drama was once again in full force. One of his bodyguards allegedly displayed a gun onstage because Tupac was arguing with some people from the audience. Concertgoers stampeded toward the exits in fear for their lives, claiming that Tupac said, "Some people might not leave here tonight because they might be dead." Two guns were later found in his dressing room, and Tupac was dropped from the Phat Rap Phest tour. As if this wasn't bad enough, four days later Milwaukee Police Officer William Robertson was shot and killed by two seventeen-year-olds. Curtis Walker and Denziss Jackson claimed that they shot the officer because they were listening to Tupac's song "Sistah Souljah." Once again, Tupac found himself involved in a controversy that had nothing to do with him directly, but would affect him publicly at a time when he didn't need this kind of attention.

Although the stakes were high, Tupac was on a mission to get his albums done. After meeting Easy Mo Bee, a producer for Biggie, at Madison Square Garden during the Budweiser Super Fest, Easy met Tupac on the set of *Above the Rim* up at Rucker Park across the street from the Polo Grounds in Harlem. Rucker Park was a main filming location.

He said come by the set. I brought my group RIP and when he got a break during sets we would go in the trailer and I played him some beats. He said I liked that but I want you to do something like Computer Love. I was thinking how many people have used this. I figured I would have to freak it. That track went into the song 'Temptations.' After the track was put together, me, my friends, and members of my group Rapping is Fundamental, AB and JR ended up singing some harmony on it. Another track he asked me about—hook me up with 'What the Telephone Bill?' by Bootsy Collins, it became the song 'Street Ballin.' Then I did a song, 'Runnin' from the Police,' which featured Tupac, Biggie, Stretch from the Live Squad, and Outlaws. We recorded this in Unique Studios on the tenth floor of what was then called studio C. I also produced another song, 'If I Died Tonight' and 'My Block' while I had an opportunity to work with him. I introduced him to my brother LG, who named himself after the housing projects where we lived, Lafayette Gardens. LG had the opportunity to produce one song for Tupac called 'Out on Bail,' which ended up on Loyal to the Game *album.*

"*It was strange too because at this time he was going back and forth to court, by day he was in court and recording at night. Studio time was at 6 P.M. at Unique Studios. When we went in the studios we recorded one batch of songs. Then he broke it down to me: 'If I Die Tonight' and 'Temptations'—I will put these two on my* Me Against the World *album. I am taking the song 'Stratight Ballin' and putting that on my* Thug Life *album. At the time Russell Simmons had the sound track for the show. We are going to put 'My*

Block' on that. 'Runnin' from the Police' ended up on the Ben Chavis Million Man March album called One Million Strong.

I am elated. I work with this dude and he puts me on four different albums. 'Runnin' from the Police' was the working title and got reduced to 'Runnin' ' as Eminem remixed it. We all know that Eminem was [there] when [Tupac and Biggie] were around and getting along. Obviously he was working with the files. They thought he was the first to put them together, what he did was work on the original tapes I recorded—if you can remember—and Eminem took Biggie and Pac out of the song and wiped everyone off and made it a Biggie and Tupac song.

I remember the recording session for 'Runnin' from the Police' in 1994 with Biggie, Pac, Stretch and my brother LG, my engineer Eric Lynch, and a couple of people from the Lafayette Gardens projects. We all had fun recording this song.

Long-time reporter and editor John-Davi Morgan reports on watchdogmilwaukee, "Isaiah Bell, 17-years-old, was shot to death during the manhunt in early September 1994, for the killers of Milwaukee police officer William Robertson." Michael McGee, the former alderman, longtime friend, and father of Ald. Michael McGee, Jr., was outraged.

The back and forth from court appearance to the studio to work on his next album would have been a taxing situation for anyone. At the time, Tupac's money was tight due to all the court cases he was facing, with little to no help from his record label. Tupac was making appearances and rapping on other people's albums to survive financially until the trial was over. Unfortunately, he would soon be asked to make an appearance on someone's album that would change his life and affect rap music forever.

FIVE

Me Against the World

Fear is stronger than love. Remember that. Fear is stronger than love. All the love I gave did me nothing when it came to fear. So it is all good. I am a soldier and I will always survive.
— TUPAC SHAKUR

As Tupac had said since his late teens, judge a man in his entirety and not for just one thing. Knowing this would not happen in a society plagued with racism, classism, and sexism, he knew that he might not receive a fair trial based on the facts and that his public persona could influence the outcome. Melissa Mourges, the assistant district attorney trying the rape case, was almost zealotlike in her persecution of Tupac.

Even while on trial, Tupac was still receiving scripts. He was sent the script for *Bullet* and decided to audition for the part of Tank. He got the part and also gained the friendship of the film's star and co-writer, Mickey Rourke. On November 6, 1994, the night before the trial was set to begin, Tupac went to Club Expo in the heart of Times Square. There he met Rourke and a friend of his, a reporter for the *Daily News* by the name of A. J. Benza. Over drinks, Tupac told Benza that he thought the rape case was a setup by Nigel, a.k.a. Jacques Agnant. Tupac also told him that Mike Tyson had warned him about Agnant, telling him he was "bad news." The account of Tupac's conversation in the *Daily News* upset Agnant when he read it.

The trial was quick despite a delay when two jurors were dismissed for making comments about disliking Tupac. The jurors were replaced when the comments were brought to his lawyer's attention. Many inconsistencies in the prosecution's case came to light during the trial. Michael Warren, Tupac's attorney, claimed that while searching the hotel room, law enforcement officials erased sexually explicit messages left by Ayanna Jackson from Tupac's voice mailbox.

On the night of November 30, while the jury was deliberating, Tupac went to a Times Square music studio, Quad Recording Studios, to rap on Little Shawn's track. Quad Studios occupies five floors of a midtown office building, so at any given time there can be a number of artists working on different projects. That night was no different. Little Shawn was recording on one floor, Biggie Small's group Junior M.A.F.I.A. was recording on another floor, while Biggie and Sean Puffy Combs were working on a video on a third.

Tupac, Stretch Walker from the Live Squad, Freddie Moore, and Zayd, Tupac's sister's boyfriend, drove to the studio. Stretch helped produce tracks for Tupac and had a hit single, "Heartless/Murderahh." They got there just after midnight and as they walked to the building, Tupac said he noticed two men in their thirties dressed in army fatigues. Neither of the men acknowledged him or his boys. He also said Little Caeser from Junior M.A.F.I.A. yelled down to him from a window in the studio, making him feel more comfortable about the situation. As he walked into the building, he noticed a third guy sitting at the desk reading a newspaper. He thought the men outside and this guy might be bodyguards for Biggie, but he was still puzzled why they didn't acknowledge him since he and Biggie were friends.

Biggie and Tupac went back a ways. They had recorded several tracks together, including "Runnin' (from the Police)" and "House of Pain." Tupac had helped Biggie start his career and let him come onstage when Tupac had concerts. Biggie even stayed at Tupac's house when he was out in L.A. Tupac had played Biggie's first single, "Party and Bullshit" all the time on the set of *Poetic Justice*. Tupac also said he gave Biggie advice about his style, advising him to change his style to attract the female audience. After that, it was said that Biggie changed his style by adding songs like "Big Poppa." So Tupac felt good about going up to the studio to see his boys.

As Tupac, Stretch, Freddie, and Zayd headed for the elevator, the three men Tupac noticed as he entered the lobby of the studio pulled out 9-millimeters and demanded that the men get to the ground and give up their jewelry. Tupac said he froze, while Stretch immediately dropped to the floor. Tupac said one of the men walked up to him and patted him down and reached for his jewelry. Tupac reflected that he saw the man's gun directed at his stomach, and by reflex he grabbed for the gun to try to direct it away from his body. During the struggle for the gun, it went off. Tupac immediately felt a burning sensation in his leg as he dropped to the floor. He then felt kicking and hitting all over his body. He lay on the ground with his eyes closed, keeping quiet as they grabbed the jewelry from his neck and hand. Then he said he felt something really strong on the back of his head. Immediately he thought he was being pistol-whipped. He could hear nothing. He felt as if everything was going white and sensed a pain in his stomach.

Tupac said the men left with his diamond ring and chains, and Freddie's jewelry. When everything calmed down, Zayd came to Tupac's side and turned him over, asking if he was all right. Although Freddie had been shot in the leg, he ran to the door and down the street after the gunmen, only to collapse on the sidewalk. Despite his injuries, Tupac managed to get upstairs to the studio with the help of Zayd and Stretch.

Tupac later described the scene at the studio to *VIBE* magazine, a scene that, to him, was unusual, to say the least:

> . . . *Andre Harrell was there, Puffy [BadBoy Entertainment CEO Sean 'Puffy' Combs] was there, Biggie . . . there was about 40 ni**as there. All of them had jewels on. More jewels than me. I*

saw Booker, and he had this look on his face like he was surprised to see me. Why? I had just beeped the buzzer and said I was coming upstairs. Little Shawn bust out crying. I went, Why is Little Shawn crying, and I got shot? He was crying uncontrollably, like, "Oh my God, Pac, you've got to sit down!" I was feeling weird, like, Why do they want to make me sit down? . . .

I didn't know I was shot in the head yet. I didn't feel nothing. I opened my pants, and I could see the gunpowder and the hole in my Karl Kani drawers. I didn't want to pull them down to see if my dick was still there. I just saw a hole and went, 'Oh sh*t. Roll me some weed.' I called my girlfriend and I was, like, 'Yo, I just got shot. Call my mother and tell her.' Nobody approached me. I noticed that nobody would look at me. Andre Harrell wouldn't look at me. I had been going to dinner with him the last few days. He had invited me to the set of New York Undercover, telling me he was going to get me a job. Puffy was standing back, too. I knew Puffy. He knew how much stuff I had done for Biggie before he came out . . .

They started telling me, "Your head! Your head is bleeding." But I thought it was just a pistol-whip. Then the ambulance came, and the police. First cop I looked up to see was the cop that took the stand against me in the rape charge. He had a half smile on his face, and he could see them looking at my balls. He said, "What's up, Tupac? How's it hanging?" . . .

When I got to Bellevue Hospital, the doctor was going, "Oh my God!" I was, like, "What? What?" And I was hearing him tell other doctors, "Look at this. This is gunpowder right here." He was talking about my head: "This is the entry wound. This is the exit wound." And when he did that, I could actually feel the holes. I said, "Oh my God. I could feel that." It was the spots that I was blacking out on. And that's when I said, "Oh sh*t. They shot me in my head." They said, "You don't know how lucky you are. You got shot five times." It was, like, weird. I did not want to believe it. I could only remember that first shot, then everything went blank.

When the EMS crew arrived, they bandaged Tupac and wheeled him down in a stretcher to waiting reporters and camera crew. He flipped the press off as he was carried into the EMS bus. The men had stolen over $40,000 worth of jewelry from Tupac and Freddie combined. Tupac was taken to Bellevue Hospital, where he underwent surgery. Dr. Leon Pachter, chief of Bellevue's trauma department, and eleven other doctors operated on the damaged blood vessel high in Tupac's right leg. On the morning of November 30, the day after the shooting, Biggie went to the hospital to check on Tupac. Tupac sent for his pastor, Herbert Daughtry, who later said, "When I arrived, Tupac looked as if he was gone. Then I said, 'Listen, son, I have come to pray for you. God is going to lift you out of this bed.' I prayed for him and then left. Our church is about thirty minutes from Bellevue Hospital and when I returned to the church one of the deacons said, 'Pastor, guess what? Have you heard about Pac? Pac got up and they can't find him.' I turned right back around. . . . "

Tupac had checked himself out of the hospital against doctors' orders. Afeni had flown up from Atlanta to be with her son and she wheeled him out the back door, through a crowd of reporters, with the Fruit of Islam (the Nation of Islam's security wing) and their old pastor from Brooklyn, the Reverend Herbert Daughtry, by her side. Tupac spent that night at the apartment of a friend, actress Jasmine Guy.

Tupac was released without bail, then an appellate court judge ordered that he be held until he could post the exorbitant bail now imposed of $3 million. Tupac's sentencing date was set for January 17, 1995, but due to his extensive injuries, the judge decided to send him back to Bellevue Hospital for medical evaluation. Based on the doctors' evaluation, he would then decide whether Tupac would remain in the hospital, or be taken to Rikers Island's prison infirmary, or be released into the general population. Tupac arrived at Bellevue at 2:00 A.M. the next day for evaluation, and went in and out of the hospital for the next week. He failed to appear at a scheduled court appearance on December 14 and the judge put out an order for him to turn himself over within twenty-four hours. It wasn't until he received a doctor's report stating that Tupac was still bleeding from his leg injury that the judge granted him another week's stay.

On February 14, 1995, amid weeping supporters, Tupac Shakur was sentenced to one and a half to four and a half years in prison for the sexual abuse of Ayanna Jackson. Tupac tearfully apologized to her, but even as he did so, he said that he had committed no crime, adding, "I hope in time you'll come forth and tell the truth." Before he received his sentence, Tupac looked directly at the judge and said, "I mean this with no disrespect, Judge—you never paid attention to me. You never looked in my eyes." He added: "You never used the wisdom of Solomon. I always felt you had something against me."

Even though Ms. Jackson said he didn't touch her, Tupac's road manager and co-defendant, Charles Fuller, was sentenced to four months in jail and five years' probation. A few months after Tupac was sentenced, Jacques Agnant pleaded guilty to two misdemeanors. The assistant district attorney who prosecuted Tupac said that Jacques was able to get more lenient treatment because Ms. Jackson was "reluctant to go through the case again." However, Ayanna Jackson wasn't reluctant enough to face a civil trial, since she filed a civil suit against Tupac immediately after the criminal trial.

Tupac was sent to Clinton Correctional Facilities in Dannemora, New York. The prison is located about five and a half hours away from New York

City and seems like it is set fifty years back in time. The archaic and depressing environment proved to diminish the once manic spirit of the Rebel of the Underground. A man who would write obsessively as an outlet for his soul was now unable to write anything at all, because the fire in his spirit was squelched.

What wasn't squelched was the fire that ignited Tupac's record sales when *Me Against the World* was propelled to the number-one spot on the Billboard album charts. Although the album was recorded before most of the drama in Tupac's life, it was very relevant to his current situation. One of the most prophetic tracks, "Fuck the World," begins, "Who you calling rapist?" and then goes on to point fingers at "devils," and "crooked cops."

Tupac still had family and friends who wrote to him daily. He also had Keisha, who would come to visit him as often as she could. On April 29, 1995, Tupac Amaru Shakur married Keisha Morris in a civil ceremony witnessed by her mother and Tupac's cousin. They talked about their future together after Tupac was released. Unfortunately, he didn't know when that was going to happen. He hadn't been granted an appeal yet and didn't have the money or assets to cover the $3 million bail the judge had set while his lawyers were appealing his case.

While in prison, Tupac started hearing rumors about who shot him. Based on the things he heard, Tupac believed that not only had Haitian Jack and William "King Tut" Johnson set him up, but Puffy and Tupac's friend Biggie were also involved. Puffy has always denied any involvement and even wrote Tupac a letter. But Tupac responded that it wasn't even like that, but as he heard the rumors it wasn't so easy to let it go. Tupac wrote about Agnant in his debut album *The Don Killuminati,* and Agnant, who has always denied working for the feds, sued him for libel.

In reaction to all the press Tupac was receiving with a number-one album and all the publicized support he received from fans and friends, Ayanna gave her version of the night's details as published on thuglifearmy.com:

> I am the young woman that was sexually assaulted by Tupac Shakur and his thugs. I've read Kevin Powell's interview with Tupac ['Ready to Live,' VIBE, April 1995], in which I was misrepresented. Up until this point I have only told my story under oath in court; nobody has heard my story, only his side, which is much different than what Tupac stated is the true story.
>
> A friend of mine took me to Nell's, where he introduced me to [the men VIBE identified as] Nigel and Trevor, who later introduced me to their friend Tupac. When I first met Tupac, he kissed me on my cheek and made small talk with me. After a while, I excused myself and started to walk to the dance floor. When I felt someone slide their hands into the back pocket of my jeans, I turned around, assuming it was my friend, but was shocked when

I discovered it was Tupac. We danced for a while, and he touched my face and his body brushed mine. Due to the small dance floor and the large number of people, we were shoved into a dark corner. Tupac pulled up his shirt, took my hand, traced it down his chest, and sat it on top of his erect penis. He then kissed me and pushed my head down on his penis, and in a brief three-second encounter, my lips touched the head of his penis. This happened so suddenly that once I realized what he was trying to do, I swiftly brought my head up. I must reiterate that I did not suck his penis on the dance floor. He pulled his shirt back down and asked me what I was doing later. I told him that I was going home because I had to go to work that day. Then, as people started surrounding him again, he grabbed my arm and said, "Let's get out of here, I'm tired of people stressing me." We exited Nell's, got into a white BMW, pulled up at the Parker Meridien, and went to his suite. We conversed, and he rolled up some blunts. We started kissing, and then we had oral and vaginal sexual intercourse several times.

He called my house a couple nights later and gave me his SkyPager number and told me he wanted to see me tomorrow. That evening after work, I paged him, and his road manager called me back and informed me that Pac really wanted to see me but he had a show to do in Jersey, so I should call a car service and take it to the Meridien and he would pay for the cab. Once I got to the hotel, I met Charles Fuller for the first time; he paid for the cab and led me upstairs. Inside the suite, Tupac, Nigel, and Trevor were seated in the living room, smoking weed and drinking Absolut. Tupac told me to come in and pointed to the arm of the sofa near him, and I sat down. After about twenty minutes, Tupac took my hand and led me into a bedroom in the suite. He fell onto the bed and asked me to give him a massage. So I massaged his back, he turned around, and I started massaging his chest.

Just as we began kissing, the door opened and I heard people entering. As I started to turn to see who it was, Tupac grabbed my head and told me, "Don't move." I looked down at him and he said, "Don't worry, baby, these are my brothers and they ain't going to hurt you. We do everything together." I started to shake my head, "No, no, Pac, I came here to be with you. I came here to see you. I don't want to do this." I started to rise up off the bed but he brutally slammed my head down. My lips and face came crashing down hard onto his penis, he squeezed the back of my neck, and I started to gag. Tupac and Nigel held me down while Trevor forced his penis into my mouth. I felt hands tearing my shoes off, ripping my stockings and panties off. I couldn't move; I felt paralyzed, trapped, and I started to black out. They leered at my body. "This bitch got a fat ass, she's fine." While they laughed and joked to one another, Nigel, Trevor, and Fuller held me in the room, trying to calm me down. They *would not allow me to leave.*

Finally, I got to the elevators, which had a panel of mirrors. Once I caught sight of myself, I sank down on the floor and started to cry. They came out, picked me up, and brought me back into the suite. Tupac was lying on the couch. In my mind I'm thinking, "This motherf*cker just raped me, and he's lying up here like a king acting as if nothing happened." So I began crying hysterically and shouting, "How could you do this to me? I came here to see you. I can't believe you did this to me." Tupac replied, "I don't have time for this shit. Get this bitch out of here."

The aforementioned is the true story. It was not a setup, and I never knew any of the thugs he was hanging with. Tupac knows exactly what he did to me. I admit I did not make the wisest decisions, but I did not deserve to be gang-raped.

Left out of her account was a statement she made as she testified. Ms. Jackson said that Agnant told her to calm down, saying that he "would hate to see what happened to Mike happen to Tupac." She knew all too well the Mike that he was referring to was Mike Tyson, who was accused of rape in Indianapolis, where he was convicted of one count of rape and two counts of deviant sexual conduct and sentenced to ten years in prison. To this day she claims she was never a part of a setup.

Having very few alternatives, Tupac asked Keisha to contact Suge Knight. Although Tupac had turned down Suge's invitation to join Death Row once before, it looked as if this time he would have to say yes. Tupac's timing was perfect because on May 11, 1995, Justice Ernst H. Rosenberger of the Appellate Division of the State Supreme Court in Manhattan decided to reduce Tupac's bail to $1.4 million from $3 million.

Prison was hard for Tupac, as it is for anyone. The guards' initial constant harassment of him and the racial slurs flung at him and the other inmates shocked Tupac deeply. Although he had talked about the abject disrespect that black men faced on a daily basis in society, he wasn't ready for the harsh realities that jail added to the equation. He was far removed from the life that he was accustomed to, and his desire for marijuana was constant. In June, Tupac was confined to his cell for sixty days for failing a drug test. He lost two months of good behavior time and privileges. Tupac was confined to his cell for eight months of his eleven-month ordeal. During that time, while Tupac wasn't able to write music, he was so accustomed to writing effortlessly that he did manage to complete a screenplay, *Live to Tell*. The screenplay is part fiction and part autobiography.

Reverend Daughtry visited. "We would talk at length. If he had a big decision to make we would go over it and I would try to be helpful. I never criticized him publicly. Instead we would talk about the decision he made about the type of future he planned for himself. I talked about the influence he had with young people. Tupac had the ability to send a message to young people greater than even the Panther Party.

Suge started to visit Tupac on a regular basis. Tupac was trying to negotiate a deal for $6 million to record three albums over three years. His latest album was number one in the country despite all the controversy and negative press, so Suge was intrigued by the deal and knew Tupac would be a great addition to Death Row. Even though the stay that the Manhattan District Attorney's office won based on Judge Rosenberger's decision prevented him from bailing out Tupac immediately, Suge began to work out a deal to make Tupac a big part of his vision for Death Row.

They worked out a handwritten contract granting Tupac the following for the first album:

- $1 million for the execution of the deal
- $125,000 for the purchase of a car
- $120,000 expense allowance for twelve months
- $250,000 legal fund to be spent through Tupac's lawyer Ogletree at Tupac's discretion
- Death Row shall secure the services of David Kenner to handle Tupac's Los Angeles cases

Tupac would then be paid a royalty of 18 points plus 1-point bumps at gold and platinum sales. In addition, for the second album, Tupac would be paid an advance of no less than $1 million, or $1 million for every million copies of the prior album that were sold, and he would be paid a royalty of 18 percent of sales plus a bonus of 1 point if it went gold, and another 1 point if it went platinum, with an amendment to the rider to have that album released in 1996. The same financial structure was set for the third album, with a rider for that album to be released in 1997.

With the terms set, agreed upon, and signed on September 15, 1995, by Suge Knight and September 16 by Tupac, Death Row lawyer David Kenner started the process of bailing Tupac out of prison. The New York Court of Appeals granted him leave to post bail. Atlantic Records raised $850,000, which was posted in a corporate guarantee. The rest was put up with a $300,000 bail bond and $250,000 in cash from Suge or Interscope. Tupac was free to start over and move forward with his career and life. After being humbled by the experience of jail, he could now make good on his words to his family to build and secure their entire future.

Tupac never lost his drive. He had a unique combination of half Panther, half rap artist that formed almost a split personality. Erica Ford and Chaz Williams were about to visit him when he was released from prison and went to Los Angeles. Chaz, who owns a record label, always thinks about what would have happened if they had been able to get Tupac out on bail and bring him back to Queens, New York.

SIX

California Love

That situation with me is like, what comes around, goes around . . . karma, I believe in karma. I believe in all of that. I'm not worried about it. They missed. I'm not worried about it unless they come back.
—TUPAC SHAKUR

Feng-Haung, Ho-oo, Firebird, Benu, and Yelit. These are the Chinese, Japanese, Russian, Egyptian, and Native American names for the phoenix, the mythical bird that rises from the ashes. Feng shui master Lam Kam Chuen talks about a bird that never dies: "It flies ahead, always scanning the landscape. It represents the capacity for vision, for collecting sensory information about events unfolding. The phoenix with its great beauty creates intense excitement and deathless inspiration."

There is something sexy and symbolic about the will of a man who has been battered by his enemies and then rises from the ashes to defeat them with his music. Tupac stated in an interview with MTV, "I was paranoid, I just got out of jail, and I've been shot, cheated, lied [to] and framed." The cuts were deep and the burns far from healed, but Tupac was ready—he was on a mission, and he was not going to be counted out.

* * *

It was Friday, October 13, 1995, and the crisp fall air hung over the Clinton Correctional Facility. Suge Knight was making final preparations for Tupac's release. Jail had suppressed Tupac's soul and kept his spirit in captivity. When he was younger, he wanted to go to jail because he thought it was some kind of rite of passage, but now this shit was real and he wanted out. The jail had become the economic engine of the predominantly white town of Clinton. Everybody worked at the jail, and the racism ran deep against its predominantly Hispanic or black population. Tupac was outraged that the guards would freely call the inmates niggers and no one seemed to mind. After David Kenner was able to post the $1.4 million for Tupac's bail, Suge arranged for a police escort and whisked Tupac onto a private plane headed to Los Angeles.

While in prison, Tupac had planned to forget the East Coast/West Coast rivalry. He even toyed with the idea of retiring from rap altogether. But then Puffy and Biggie retaliated with an interview responding to Tupac's jailhouse story. All parties named in Tupac's *VIBE* interview were contacted for comment, but chose not to participate. After the article was published, Biggie demanded an apology and denied involvement; Puffy stated "he [Tupac] got a lot of people in some bullshit with that interview. Nobody turned their back on him. The way it was written it was open-ended, like me and Big and Andre Harrell had something to do with it. I would never purposely ever try to hurt the next man."

Tupac felt that they had twisted the facts in their rebuttal interview and he became incensed. He was now even more relentless and enraged.

When he arrived in sunny California he felt free; it was good to be home. Tupac conducted a few interviews, managed to get some errands done, then headed straight for Cam-Am studios and began recording his next album. He worked at a feverish pace, writing lyrics even when he went to the bathroom. Some of his songs were harder than before, and he rapped as if he were on a mission of vengeance. Maybe his drive to record this new music was influenced by Death Row and Suge's gangsta style; maybe it reflected his bitterness about being set up in the rape case or being shot by people who he thought were his friends. Or perhaps it was a result of his disappointment with being abandoned in jail.

Regardless of what fueled his soul, Tupac had stepped right into an East Coast/West Coast feud that escalated into a full-out, mostly media war between two coasts of musical geniuses. Tupac would let his music fan the flames.

Tupac married Keisha on April 29, 1995, but he wasn't ready for marriage, and the union was soon annulled. Tupac claimed he still loved Keisha and that she would always have a place in his heart. When he got out of prison, being the young, sexy, rich man that he now was, he could date any woman he wanted, and he chose a woman named Tiffany as one of the women he would see.

Tiffany, a drop-dead slender bombshell, had a reputation for dating some of the richest and most powerful men in music and the streets. She was their confidante and lover, with the looks of a model and the knowledge of a street hustler. Tiffany had honey-colored hair to match her honey-toned skin. At the age of twenty-two she was a statuesque beauty. She fell in love with the fast lifestyle and the men that were a part of it, two of whom were Biggie and Tupac. Tiffany first met Tupac shortly after the March 1996 Mike Tyson vs. Frank Bruno fight in Las Vegas. She recalls, "I was with four girls including my sister. We stayed in Las Vegas an extra couple of days and now were booked to leave on the red-eye flight that night back to New York. We headed over to the Luxor, because we heard they had rides and shit. We were walking around the pool area and my sister said, 'Oh shit, there goes Suge Knight!' Then we noticed he had Tupac and some members of the Dogg Pound with him. We headed right over to them and out of the group one of them said 'what is poppin'?'

"We started talking, taking pictures and hugging nicely; when it was my turn Tupac grabbed me by my ass and said 'we are having a party back at the house.' I said, 'But we are leaving out to head back to New York.'

"'Baby, I am a millionaire, you have nothing to worry about. You are with me.'

"Shit, he turned me on and I was ready to give him head right there out in the open. It was something about him; maybe it was this magnetism about him, all I knew was that I wanted him."

They went back to the house. It was crazy. The house was huge. Tiffany said there were a million niggas inside smoking blunts and on the outside there were niggas playing cards. A chef was cooking for everybody, and Tupac and Tiffany just hung out and relaxed.

Tiffany described the scene: "Tupac was tired and went upstairs and slept for a few hours. I stayed in my lane and mad bitches started coming. The living room is huge and there are four couches and there are sets of girls all waiting to see who he will choose. When Tupac came downstairs he sat right next to me and the women were just waiting to see who he was going to.

"He sat next to me for hours. It was a wild sexy atmosphere and the other girls would say come over here and he let them know I am with my people and I am good. We talked for hours and he told me and my friends how he had fucked Faith, Biggie's wife."

This was right after the story broke in the media in February 1996. Faith denied it vehemently. A talented writer and singer, Faith Evans had married Biggie Smalls after less than three weeks of courtship. She held her own, but her marriage was under the strain of both her and Biggie pursuing their careers and being on the road. Still, she loved him. Faith claimed that she met Tupac while she was in Los Angeles writing for a group called The Truth. She did a rough vocal pending BadBoy's approval. Within no time a song was released that Death Row claimed was by Jewell, but it was Faith's vocals and she became the center of the East Coast/West Coast firestorm.

Tiffany continued, "The bitches started trickling out and we started smoking weed. When it was time to go to sleep he said you are sleeping with me right. I said no doubt. The sex was fucking out of this world. We smashed all night, he had me bent over the terrace, he gave me oral sex and I gave him oral sex and he even took off the condom and said I don't even care. While we were fucking he said you have 'some nigger in New York who would kill over this shit.' I was with a dude who eventually tried to kill me when he found out I was with Tupac. Chasing me down Lenox Avenue, attacking me at the airport and even staging a robbery of my house and holding my shit hostage because he felt rejected. But that is another story. Tupac had the maid bring breakfast in bed and poured mimosas on his dick while I sucked it. That night girls came from Los Angeles and I know how to hold my lane so I left. We never exchanged numbers and I was devastated. The next week I saw Suge Knight at the Mirage nightclub and he said 'my man got an APB on you. Do not even go to your house, he needs you in L.A., just go to the Four Seasons and we will take care of you and your five girls.' Shit, I jumped in the limo. Suge dropped off money for me and my girls to go shopping and we were off to L.A. We went to the mall to all the best shops and went to Pac's album release party at the Air Museum.

"There were mad bitches in the party. One thing that I understand about this nasty game is that you have to wait your turn. We saw one another. I was wearing a white dress and he pulled me close and we danced to 'Your Body Is Calling Me.' I understood that he had prior commitments before I jumped into the picture. He liked me so much he just threw me in the mix. I knew I was not his main bitch. Norris his assistant told me that Tupac must really like fucking with you because he fly you in because Death Row had bitches on the payroll. Everyone had a pussy bill, even Suge.

"Tupac took really good care of me and I spent three weeks with him in L.A. I sat on a stool right next to him in the booth as he recorded 'Hit Em Up.' He wanted me to get on the track and I couldn't, I lived in New York. That night Gip and Joia came with their baby, Johnny J was there, Daz was in the studio working, and Krupt was in and out. Left Eye came to the studio with a group of girls that looked like dykes to me and was giving us the evil eye. Lisa and Pac fucked around and she was pissed off at me because both Pac and I would go to the bathroom together in between recording sessions. All he wanted me to do was give him oral sex for breakfast, lunch, and dinner. He did five songs in one night and recorded part of *Makaveli*.

"What was great about Tupac was we would sit up all night and talk. We did that on several occasions. He consumed me and would give me his undivided attention. He loved and wanted to be loved. It was beautiful and we grew closer. We would talk about every issue under the sun from world issues, politics, and things that really bothered him. He loved black people and could not stand to see them suffer; he was a man of the people. He also had a lot of curiosity about the niggas from New York and would ask questions about the ones that I knew from the streets. During my visits he said to me one time, 'Tiff, why don't you get a tattoo that says 100 percent Tupac on your back.' I laughed and told Tupac do not get carried away. I knew the Tupac that was sensitive, loving, caring, and had passion for the people. But I also witnessed the 'I will gut a nigga out' side of him, and that shit was scary.

"On my last visit with him to L.A. he said, 'Look, me and Kidada is rocking and that is my people so I am going to have to let you go.' He gave me a parting gift and that was it. I was shattered. I went from drinking Cristal, Louis, and lunch at Spago's to hearing this shit. He gave me a wonderful parting gift. The last time I saw Tupac his assistant Norris called me during the MTV Music Awards in August of 1996. Tupac was in New York, my city, and we hung out. There was no sex, just you my peoples and I love you, I fucked with your vibe. We had a great time and he gave me some money as he always did and I said my good-byes. Tupac was a man of the people and I had to let him go."

Ironically, Tiffany and Biggie were digging each other too. Cuda, a music manager, introduced them. Tiffany says, "I was fucking with Cuda at the time, Biggie and I had a big blowout. Cuda was hating because Biggie and I were attracted to each other and he cock-blocked. Later on it was me who spent the last week of Biggie's life with him in L.A. and on the day I left Biggie was killed."

Tupac found a rose in Kidada Jones. Kidada is the daughter of Quincy Jones, whom he first met after attacking Quincy and his family in the press in 1993 for marrying white actress Peggy Lipton. Quincy Jones's youngest daughter, Rashida, wrote a letter refuting Tupac's accusations against her family and wanted to celebrate that in fact she was biracial. When Kidada was at a party, Tupac ran after her thinking it was Rashida, wanting to apologize for his remarks about her father. Kidada kept wondering why he was following her. Then she remembered the article. When they met, the friendship turned into chemistry and they simply became two people in love. One day Quincy Jones took Rashida to meet Kidada at a restaurant in Los Angeles and reached over to the booth behind him and said, "TUPAC!" Tupac was startled, and Quincy asked Tupac to come and talk to him in the corner. Quincy told him how much his remarks had hurt his family. Tupac apologized privately as well as publicly. Kidada was important to Tupac; she stabilized him.

Tupac recorded enough songs to fulfill his Death Row deal within a few short months and still had over two hundred tracks left. He noticed that not everything was as it seemed at Death Row. He was relieved that back in February his friend Snoop Dogg (Calvin Broadus), twenty-four, and his former body-guard, McKinley Lee, twenty-six, were found not guilty of first- and second-degree murder and conspiracy to commit assault in the 1993 shooting of Philip Woldemariam, a twenty-year-old Ethiopian immigrant and gang member in Los Angeles. He'd been told earlier on that all labelmate Dr. Dre needed to do was testify in Snoop's murder trial, because the witness was lying. All Dr. Dre had to say was that Snoop was never in the car from which the shots were fired in order to prove Snoop's innocence. Dre never showed up in court because he was too busy.

Cracks began to be seen in the once tight Death Row facade. In early 1996, when Death Row was devoting itself to Tupac's first Death Row album, *All Eyez on Me,* Dr. Dre was contemplating leaving the label. "At first it was just a big family thing," he says. "But the more money that got made, the further apart everybody came. It's like, certain people started becoming what they hated." He adds:

"I wasn't feeling comfortable with the people I was around. Everybody wasn't professional. I always wanted things at Death Row to be right and positive, because I'm a positive person. And the situation I was in wasn't, plain and simple. It was too much negativity. Most likely, there are gonna be records coming out dissing me, dissing people I've worked with and am going to be working with. It's just a lot of negative bullshit. So from here on out, Death Row Records don't even exist to Dre."

It has also been said that Dre was upset that Suge used "California Love" for *All Eyez on Me,* when the song was slated to be on Dre's upcoming album. DMaq had created the song's remix version beat for

Dr. Dre. He says, "When Tupac heard the joint he said I got to have this joint on my album. Years later Suge, Dr. Dre, and a team of people came together at the table to sort it out and I finally got the credit on the song. I must thank Afeni Shakur, who made sure that things were straightened out and also opened up opportunities for so many producers who worked on Tupac's music."

Dre left Death Row to start up his own label, Aftermath, which was also distributed by Interscope. Tupac's version and Dre's version of why he left Death Row of course differed. Tupac said he got Dre pushed off the label. He said, "Suge is the boss of Death Row, the don. But I'm the underboss, the capo. That's my job, to do what's best for all of Death Row. My decision wasn't based on comin' to Death Row and taking shit over. My decision was based on Dre not being there for Snoop during his trial. Also, other niggas was producing beats, and Dre was gettin' the credit. And I got tired of that. He was owning the company too and he chillin' in his house. I'm out here in the streets, whoopin' niggas' asses, startin' wars and shit, droppin' albums, doin' my shit, and this nigga takin' three years to do one song." He also said, "Dre is doing his own thing. It doesn't affect us. My take on what happened was that Snoop went on trial for murder for his life. Somebody said Dre was in the car. The jury believed that we needed Dre to be able to say he wasn't there, once they would've saw that he wasn't there that would've saved Snoop's whole case. Dre never showed up. He said he was too busy. I don't wanna be a part of him or around him. Plus I feel that what was done in the dark will come to light. There are secrets that everybody's gonna find out about."

Dre did eventually become a target of Tupac's venomous words as he had predicted. On his *The Don Killuminati: The 7 Day Theory,* Tupac recorded under the name Makaveli, he says Dre's reign is over and even goes on to question his sexuality.

Tupac never let the public see his enthusiasm waver for Death Row. He was always out in front like a soldier. He talked publicly about how great it was to be on Death Row, how much they gave him. Publicly, Death Row was like his family, but what was going on behind the scenes was right out of a movie about the most dysfunctional family imaginable.

Although Suge Knight treated Tupac like a brother, this did not stop Death Row Records from participating in financial improprieties against Tupac. Several years later these improprieties would show up in a lawsuit that Afeni Shakur filed against Death Row Records.

Tupac had a plan. He fired Death Row's lawyer, David Kenner, who also represented him in all of his business affairs. Death Row had served its purpose, and Tupac had had enough. Finally he was going to take control of his own destiny.

SEVEN

Hail Mary

Dear mama don't cry; Your baby boy's doin' good; Tell the homies I'm in heaven and it ain't got hoods
—TUPAC SHAKUR

I Ain't Mad at Cha, the last video in which Tupac appeared, was made about a month before his death and was delivered to MTV just three days after he died. The video has eerie similarities to Tupac's own demise. It depicts Tupac with a friend, played by actor Bokeem Woodbine, being ambushed, getting shot several times, and then dying in an ambulance. He is then brought into heaven and greeted by such black American entertainment greats as guitarist Jimi Hendrix, jazz legends Miles Davis and Louis Armstrong, blues singer Billie Holiday, and trailblazing actor and comedian Redd Foxx.

Tupac did not want to go to Las Vegas, but had given his word to perform at Club 662, a local hot spot owned by businesswoman Helen Thomas, president of Platinum Road Inc. Coincidentally, 662 spells M.O.B. on a telephone keypad, which is the acronym for Suge's reputed gang affiliation. The evening's event would include performances by Run DMC and others after Tyson's fight with Bruce Seldon that evening. Tupac's performance was arranged by Suge to easily fulfill Tupac's community service requirements culminating from one of his many open cases. The concert would serve to benefit a local boxing organization.

Barry's Boxing Center, a haven for the young who seek a father figure, direction, and discipline, is run by former professional boxer Pat Barry and his wife, Dawn. Dawn was one of the first female professional boxing managers and is now a retired Las Vegas Metro Police Officer. Pat is still active with LVMPD, where he has been a detective for over twenty-five years. The Boxing Center, located at 2664 South Highland, prides itself on being a nonprofit organization developed to encourage young men and women in their pursuit of excellence in the sport of boxing both in and out of the ring. The center's motto is "we teach the science, not the violence." Although Barry did not know Tupac or Suge Knight personally, their appearance was arranged by then club lawyer George Keleiss. Coincidentally, Suge had an interest in purchasing the club and arranged for celebrities to attend the event.

Six months earlier, Tupac was ringside and witnessed the comeback of Mike Tyson against Frank Bruno at the Luxor Hotel. He had written two songs for Mike, and they were used as his theme songs as Tyson entered the ring. Tupac and Mike had similar backgrounds, and both used their passion and talents to garner them fame and fortune. Mike had had his run-in with the law from a rape case and had served time in an Indiana penitentiary.

Mike, too, had grown up poor, sometimes home-less, without a father, and was an outcast in his beloved Brownsville, Brooklyn. Despite the demons that haunted him, the outspoken boxer with a fierce temper was generous to a fault, and rose to be one of the greatest fighters of his era.

Tupac and Kidada arrived in Las Vegas about 2:00 P.M. and checked into their hotel room at the Luxor, just one block away from the MGM Grand. Frank Alexander, Tupac's personal bodyguard, joined him on this trip. Alexander, a former reserve officer, was given this position after an incident in which he safely led Snoop and other members of Death Row from the path of a hail of bullets. Someone had begun shooting into the Winnebago on the set of the Dogg Pound video *New York, New York* in Red Hook, Brooklyn. Once one of the most notorious neighborhoods in New York, the area was bordered by the waters of the East River and iso-lated among warehouses, Red Hook public hous-ing projects, and shipping ports.

Tupac dismissed the rest of his bodyguard detail when he hired Frank. They spent an enormous amount of time together, and if Tupac was in the vicinity, Frank was right behind him. A series of unusual events occurred around Death Row's visit to Las Vegas. Several out-of-state security guards would be part of the Death Row security detail. When the guards arrived they were called in by Wrightway Security, a firm utilized by Death Row Records, for their first and last security meeting. It was unusual for the security team to have team meetings, but they sat and listened. The guards were disappointed to find out that the firm was unable to obtain the necessary permits for them to carry firearms. If they were caught with any guns, they could face stiff penalties and even jail time. Advised by Suge's attorney, they left their firearms behind, but made a plan among themselves that they would leave the guns in the car in the parking lot. If needed, they would be able to retrieve them at any time.

While the main attraction for the night, the Mike Tyson fight, began at 8:00 P.M., Club 662 already had a line with people paying $75 as early as 5:00 P.M. to ensure entry to the event. Suge and Tupac, along with their guests, sat ringside and in classic Tyson style, the fight lasted a mere 109 seconds, leaving Seldon knocked out in the first round. Afterward, as they were exiting the garden arena at about 8:30, Orlando "Baby Lane" Anderson, a twenty-two-year-old who was an alleged well-known Crip gang member from Compton, California, was pointed out to Tupac. Some say Anderson bore a slight resemblance to Tupac.

Three months prior, Orlando was rumored to have stolen a Death Row medallion at a California mall, personally given to one of Death Row's members as a gift from Suge. Travon Lane, who was alleged to be that member, pointed out Orlando. Tupac immediately strode over to Anderson and asked, "Are you from the south?" Before he could even respond, Tupac punched him in the face.

In an article in *VIBE* magazine, Anderson could not remember if Tupac said anything; all he said he could recall was that he felt like he was "being swarmed." The surveillance tape showed him being stomped, punched, and kicked by the members of Death Row, including Tupac and Suge. Anderson was seen walking away visibly bleeding and shaken, but refused medical assistance or to file a complaint offered by hotel security. Although the hotel responded to the incident and had the ruckus on tape, there was no incident report filed, nor were the police called.

Tupac returned to the Luxor to change his clothes, and with the crew in tow, headed to Suge's house so that Suge could do the same. Suge Knight had a palatial home on Monte Rosa Avenue in the Paradise Valley Township. After all, Las Vegas was partly his town; he was a resident and knew the town well from his days as a star football player for the University of Las Vegas Rebels. Some say Tupac thought it was too hot and the bulletproof vest he was always known to wear was too bulky to wear under his basketball jersey—a choice that later proved to be fatal. The group left Suge's house at around 10:00 P.M.

Frank decided to drive Kidada's Lexus, leaving his own car back at the Luxor Hotel with his gun. He was the only bodyguard with the group, and he was unarmed. There were extra police hired to cover Suge's residence, and there was another group awaiting them at Club 662.

While the group cruised the strip on the way to Club 662, the air was filled with excitement as a parade of flashy cars and limousines snaked down the streets. The brand-new BMW stereo system of the 750i was blaring, with a bass that made you feel the music in your chest. Around the corner from Bally's Casino, Suge and Tupac were stopped by a bicycle patrol officer for loud music and improperly displayed license plates. They were not cited and were released a few minutes later. In Sin City, it was unusual for a stop not to be noted and a ticket not issued for these offenses.

At 11:15 P.M., the caravan of cars was just blocks away from Club 662 when a late-model white Cadillac slowly rolled up alongside the BMW as Suge and Tupac sat at a red light. There, someone that Frank Alexander described as a black man with a knit cap fitted close to his head tracked his gun, and then fired off at least thirteen rounds at Tupac, who sat in the front passenger's seat.

As the shots rang through the car, Tupac tried to get to the backseat, and Suge said he pulled Tupac down in an attempt to shield him with his own body. The sound of glass and shrapnel pierced the night, bystanders fled, and chaos ensued. The Cadillac sped away and made a right turn on Koval Lane at a green light. The choice of car was key, as there were hundreds of white limousines and cars along the strip.

Tupac was hit four times. One bullet became lodged in his chest. The second bullet went through his hip bone and rested in his pelvic area, and the third sliced his right hand. Suge was grazed by a bullet in his neck area and hit with flying glass and debris. Although injured, Suge stated that Tupac was alert, and Suge was concerned for him because it appeared that he'd been shot in the head. Then Tupac's breathing became shallow and he was losing blood.

Frank Alexander, in shock, ran up to the front of the BMW and was amazed when Suge suddenly made a U-turn, with two tires on his car already blown out by gunshots. He could not believe that anyone was still alive. Drivers and pedestrians were in a daze, and drove or walked over to the crime scene as two bicycle patrolmen chose to follow the BMW instead of calling for immediate backup to catch the car while they secured the scene and gathered the now scattering witnesses. That decision would prove to be detrimental to the case.

Instead of heading to Desert Springs Hospital, which was in the near vicinity, Suge bobbed and weaved through traffic, heading back to the Strip. His car finally came to a halt after getting caught at a median a few blocks away from the crime scene. Immediately the Strip lit up like a Christmas tree with police officers, ambulances, and members of the fire and rescue squads when the car came to a halt. Every available unit in the city responded to the bicycle cops' belated appeal for backup. Police reached the car on the Strip, where it was caught in traffic at Harmon Avenue.

In the confusion, the police, not sure what had happened, held everyone at gunpoint. The officers were shouting, "Get down!" Everyone was told to sit on the sidewalk with their hands on their heads. Frank Alexander, who was stuck at a light a half block back, witnessed Suge being held at gunpoint facedown on the pavement. After everything was sorted, Tupac was lifted into the ambulance along with Suge to be taken to University Medical Center. Frank, who unsuccessfully tried to get into the ambulance, could hear Tupac saying, "I'm a dying man."

At the hospital, Tupac underwent the first of three operations. His right lung was removed to stop internal bleeding. According to Cathy Scott, a reporter for the *Las Vegas Sun* and author of *The Killing of Tupac Shakur*, "When Tupac arrived at University Medical Center immediately following the shooting, a trauma center surgeon removed one bullet from Tupac's pelvic area." Tupac's injuries included a gunshot wound to his right chest with a massive hemothorax, and a gunshot wound to the right thigh with the bullet palpable within the abdomen. Tupac also had a gunshot wound to a right finger with a fracture. The preoperative diagnosis was a gunshot wound to the chest and abdomen, and there was postoperative bleeding. The bullet in Tupac's chest was not removed during surgery, but during the autopsy, Coroner Ron Flud told Scott. It then became evidence. When Tupac arrived at the hospital's trauma center, he was wheeled into the recovery area and "was resuscitated" and a "full trauma activation was called."

He was placed on life support machines. Two liters of blood that had hemorrhaged into his chest cavity were removed. Tupac's pulse was "very thready and initially he had a minimal blood pressure, which rapidly declined." He was taken immediately to the operating room for surgical intervention and further resuscitation.

Tupac then underwent two more operations. The first started at 6:25 P.M. on September 8 and lasted an hour. The surgery consisted of exploratory procedures. The surgeon noted that it appeared Tupac had had some prior surgery for bullet wounds in his upper right chest area. The second operation consisted of ligation of bleeding and removal of a bullet from his pelvic area.

Friends and fans held a vigil for Tupac outside of the hospital. Yafeu "Kadefi" Fula, who was part of the rap group the Outlawz, was part of the caravan of cars behind the black BMW that night. He cooperated with the police and after questioning made his way to the hospital, but not before calling his mother to tell her to let Afeni Shakur know that Tupac had been shot. After receiving the call the following morning, Afeni got on the first flight to Las Vegas with her daughter and cousin Deena in tow.

Suge Knight was released from University Medical Center on Sunday, September 8. On that same day, Tupac underwent another procedure to repair damage from the bullet wounds. On Monday, September 9, it was reported that Las Vegas Metro Police and about twenty friends and fans of Shakur were in an altercation over what police called a "misunderstanding." Tensions were calmed with help from a female friend of Tupac's, and four men handcuffed during the scuffle were released. No one was arrested.

On Wednesday, September 11, Suge, accompanied by his attorneys, spoke about the shooting to Metro Police for about an hour. Billy Garland, who was rumored to be Tupac's biological father, showed up at the hospital to sit by Tupac's bedside. He had no money for a hotel room and a very good friend of Tupac's, a video director, willingly shared his hotel room.

On Friday, September 13, 1996, after several successful attempts at resuscitating Tupac after his heart repeatedly stopped, doctors were ordered by Tupac's mother not to resuscitate him if his heart stopped again. Tupac Amaru Shakur was pronounced dead by Dr. James Lovett at University Medical Center at 4:03 P.M. After Tupac was pronounced deceased, no one other than family was allowed in his room.

Later that evening at 7:00, the coroner's medical examiner performed an autopsy on Tupac's body, and at around 9:00 P.M. his body was released to Davis Mortuary. At the request of Afeni Shakur, he was cremated. On Saturday, September 14, Afeni Shakur received the remains of her beloved son. She left Las Vegas the same day with her family and has never returned.

EIGHT

Life of an Outlaw

I believe that everything that you do bad comes back to you. So everything that I do that's bad, I'm going to suffer from it. But in my mind, I believe what I'm doing is right. I feel like I'm going to go to heaven.
— TUPAC SHAKUR

Tupac knew at an early age that he would be a revolutionary. In fact, he was raised by Afeni Shakur and her fellow Panthers to be a Black Prince. The theories of empowerment and Black Power became a part of his soul. His mother told him stories of her own revolutionary acts, and although his family's lineage read like the *Who's Who* of America's most wanted, Tupac knew that they sacrificed their lives for the betterment of the community. He also knew that he bore the responsibility of picking up where they left off. Yet while he felt compelled to follow in their hard-fought footsteps, Tupac felt conflicted. Where were his mother's Panther brothers and sisters when she needed them most, when they were homeless, when she carried the torch by herself, when she turned to drugs to ease her pain and he was left to wonder why? There were many reasons for Afeni's pain that the child could not see or comprehend until he became a man. The downfall of the Panther Party, her own brushes with the law, and having to raise her son and daughter alone are just a few things that could have led her down a self-destructive path. Regardless, Tupac felt betrayed by the very people he so admired. Still, he honored and believed in the revolutionary principles that influenced his elders, and he espoused them in his lyrics. Sometimes these very same principles were the cause of the scorn he felt from society in general.

When Erica Ford heard about Tupac's death she was greatly saddened. She says, "I felt that hip-hop and young people really lost a giant. I think about what the music industry would have been if Tupac was still alive.

"We remembered Tupac's life with numerous services and memorials but we did a huge event in Queens with Treach, Kid Capri, and Tupac's extended family members. From that event people became interested in building again, building The Code again. We developed the work on a musical code, open mic, panel discussions, and Tupac was the inspiration for the Million Youth March that took place on September 5, 1998. Over 100,000 young people filled the streets of Harlem speaking out on police brutality and the issues that were affecting their communities.

"Tupac had intelligence; he was not about being ignorant but about gaining knowledge, every day. His work continues with The Code Foundation, where we tirelessly work with young people on how to get a job, career choices, and present positive images. Tupac's influence continues with rapper Ja

Rule. We have taken the concept of The Code with the development of Life Sports Camp (Love Ignites Freedom through Education). For more information visit www.Lifesportscamp.org or call (718) 739-1596."

Contrary to the good things Tupac set into motion, as his fame grew, so did Tupac's wild-child reputation. Pac had become an enemy of the state; his music had become an anthem for the ghettos, barrios, and villages of the world whose inhabitants were disenfranchised and without hope. Here in America, politicians publicly challenged his lyrics but were hard-pressed not to agree that he had a point. Urban communities were gripped with poverty, joblessness, drugs, teen pregnancy, gang violence, homelessness, and rising rates of black men in jail. Tupac's music gave the reason why, in graphic detail. The picture he painted was of young disenfranchised and impoverished youth who were starving socially, emotionally, financially, and politically, and were ready for change. He said, "If we are hungry we are going to knock." As in his life and with his death, Tupac's knock was heard loud and clear.

It is not unusual for musicians who die at the height of their careers to become cultlike heroes, as was the case with Jimi Hendrix and Kurt Cobain, but no one could have predicted the success or the phenomenon of Tupac Shakur. Within one week of Tupac's death, sales of *All Eyez on Me,* which was released February 13, 1996, tripled. Two weeks after his death the album went from number 69 to number 6 on the *Billboard* pop chart. Sales continued to rise, with 76,000 units sold by the week of September 22, 1996. During the week of October 6, 1996, the album sold 62,000 copies. *The Don Killuminati: The 7 Day Theory,* released November 5, 1996, debuted at number 1 on the charts.

Tupac Shakur sold more records than any rapper in 2001, five years after his death. The album *Until the End of Time* went triple platinum with very little promotion and a release of just one single. In 2002, Tupac's second posthumous album, *Better Dayz,* debuted at number 5 with 366,000 copies; it has sold 1.6 million to date.

In December 2004, *Billboard* magazine reported that Tupac's third posthumous chart topper, *Loyal to the Game* (Amaru/Interscope), entered the charts at number 1, selling 3,330,000 copies. Tupac's albums had sold 18 million units in the United States, with a career total of 24.4 million. In the same year, eight years since his death, Tupac Shakur entered the *Guinness Book of World Records* as the bestselling rap/hip-hop artist ever, having sold more than 67 million albums worldwide, 37 million records in the United States alone (mostly posthumously). Tupac has consistently been voted by fans and critics alike as the greatest rapper of all time.

On the commemoration of the tenth anniversary of his death, Tupac "participated" in a world tour. This time, it was Tupac's fifty-five-pound wax replication that had the starring role in Madame Tussaud's wax museum in Las Vegas, the same city in which he was killed. The exhibit, called "Tupac

Eternal," depicted a shirtless replica of the artist, sporting a bandanna and proudly displaying all of his tattoos. The exhibit will visit cities such as New York, Hong Kong, and London. Seven hundred hours were dedicated to bringing Tupac's wax portrait to life. Jeni Fairey of Madame Tussaud's of London utilized a slew of photographs provided by Afeni Shakur.

After Tupac's death, a younger generation of rap-hungry teens who were not aware of Tupac's music made a stampede to the record stores. His death and the mystery and controversy that clouded his life have ironically given him heightened popularity among the younger generation. *VIBE* magazine asked, "Why is it that we cannot stop thinking about Tupac Amaru Shakur and Christopher 'The Notorious B.I.G.' Wallace? Why do we still care? Why do we not only care, but are in many cases obsessed?" Like many cultural icons, they died young, in their prime and at the apex of their careers. And their murders remain unsolved, adding to the mystique—Why were they killed? Who killed them? Why did they have to die? With such unanswered questions, the public will remain intrigued. What makes Tupac unique is that he was so prolific in his writing, and many of his songs are yet to be released. His music—new music—will continue to entertain and educate, and to enlarge his legend.

"People often ask why Tupac had so much more material than other artists, specifically Biggie. He was a lot more than just a rapper, he was a voice of a lot of people who were disenfranchised, who did not have an opportunity," states Jac Benson, an executive producer who spent most of his life documenting rap in such shows as *YO MTV Raps!* "Tupac was the voice of hip-hop; he spent a lot of time talking, preaching, and making himself a martyr to a degree. Tupac also spent a great deal of time in the studio and recorded hundreds of songs. Whenever you read he was in trouble, Tupac spent even more time recording things that were relevant to him and reflected his experiences as a young black man in America. Every time [his estate] releases an album, it is like he is still here. Fortunately, Tupac's music is timeless. You will find some artists will put out a Christmas album or a best-of album. Tupac's stuff is still new material that most of the world has not heard. His music still competes with the best rappers of today. People will forever speak volumes of his talents. Tupac worked with some of the best producers and coupled with his talent gave his voice a great sound."

Havelock Nelson, the first rap editor for *Billboard* (1991–98), and author of *Bring the Noise: A Guide to Rap Music and Hip-Hop Culture*, recalls, "Tupac Shakur had immaculate phrasing. I'm not talking about his rhyme flow, but the way he moved and carried himself. His swagger communicated unadulterated charisma and authenticity. He was way past cool without ever trying too hard. This was his transcendent characteristic: realness.

"Pac's indelible presence hit me the moment I first

met him. I was introduced to him in a crowded Oakland club, before he was making headlines. But the impression he left lasted. I'm sure he'd encountered millions of people in his lifetime and had the same effect on all of them.

"From that initial meeting I was fascinated by Tupac's directness, the way he did and said bold things without ever apologizing. Pac was no fool, and whenever he reflected on his actions—no matter how insane they seemed on the surface—his explanations were coherent and presented without hypocrisy. They anchored our collective understanding of his complex personality. He always kept things interesting, which was golden, and this is what made Tupac immortal."

Although his popularity has grown since his murder, while he was alive, Tupac had a large—and loyal—fan base. Tupac's songs spoke of the day-to-day lives of so many kids. Songs like "Brenda Had a Baby," and "Keep Your Head Up" made them feel he was talking about them, telling the world about their lives and struggles and not to count them out. Tupac touched people in a sincere way and when he died, his fans felt as though they'd lost a loyal friend, even a relative. "His death made his fans embrace him even more," recalls rap legend Big Daddy Kane. "Tupac also inspired brotherhood among his friends, a special bond that became infectious as Tupac would say, 'If I fuck with you I fuck,' a slogan for his loyalty to whom he deemed were friends. His friends felt the same way about him."

Kane remembers, "I was driving from Greensboro, North Carolina, to New York and pulled into a gas station in Richmond, Virginia, to fill up on gas. Someone recognized me and said 'Are you going to the Tupac concert?' I asked where it was and immediately turned my car around and headed for the venue."

But just as Tupac had a duality in his life and persona, the flip side seemed to follow him in death. As his popularity grew worldwide, the mystery surrounding his death and the events that led up to it began the unraveling of Death Row Records. Tupac unsuspectingly had become embroiled in a war that involved greed, shady figures, and power. The code of the streets requires no snitching. America was shocked when in an interview on *Prime Time Live*, Suge Knight was asked whether he would tell the police if he knew who killed Tupac. Suge's reply was, ". . . absolutely no. I do not get paid to solve homicides."

As the days went on, so did the divulging of the bizarre, and at times nefarious, goings-on at Death Row. It seems Knight had long arms, arms that hugged some in law enforcement a little too close for judicial liking. Even before the death of Tupac, Death Row was involved in much drama. The *Los Angeles Times* reported in October 1996 that Suge Knight had awarded a recording contract to the daughter of Deputy District Attorney Lawrence Longo, who helped work out a probation deal in an assault against Knight filed by two brothers whom he'd beaten with a telephone.

The Associated Press reported that Gina Longo, eighteen, said she had been unfairly linked to a controversy involving Knight and her father. Gina, who has studied dance and singing since age six, defended her contract at Death Row. She is the first white performer at the rap label and said Knight once commented he was impressed with her "voice and look." "I'm no Milli Vanilli," said Longo, referring to the pop duo that lost a Grammy award after it was discovered they had lip-synced their 1990 debut album. "The reason I'm on Death Row has nothing to do with my dad. I got my deal because I can sing. I know the perception out there is that everything was just handed to me on a silver platter, but that's not the way it went down. I'm my own person and I got my own contract." She signed a multi-album deal with Death Row in January of 1996, worth an estimated $50,000. Gina Longo never ended up recording an album to be released by Death Row.

It was also found that Death Row lawyer David Kenner rented from the Longo family a $19,000-a-month Malibu home in which Suge had stayed. The district attorney was pulled from the case and investigated for the apparent conflict of interest. Then the *Los Angeles Times* reported that Steve Cantrock, an accountant for Death Row and a representative of Gelfand, Rennert & Feldman (a division of Coopers & Lybrand), signed a document stating that he'd stolen $4.5 million from Death Row. Cantrock told federal investigators he had been forced onto his knees and made to sign the confession that Kenner had written on the spot. Suge Knight denied this, and Cantrock denied stealing the money.

In the events leading up to Tupac's death, Suge went to trial for breaking probation and for participating in the beating of Orlando Anderson that fateful night in Las Vegas. In what was becoming a usual twist with witnesses who testified in a Suge Knight case, Anderson changed his story on the witness stand and testified in defense of Suge. In 1996, Knight was sentenced to five years in prison for violating his probation for an assault and weapons conviction in 1992.

Outside of the courtroom there was another war heating up—this one corporate, not criminal. Enter the Tupac–Death Row merger. On the heels of the battle between Time Warner, who had come under fire, Interscope had used the opportunity of a somewhat desperate Tupac in jail to arrange for him to join Death Row. As the story goes, Suge Knight visited Tupac in jail, promising him his freedom and a chance to record again. Tupac is said to have taken to Suge like an older brother or father figure. The deal between them was rumored to have been signed on a piece of toilet tissue. Signing Tupac was a coup for Death Row, which was then a young company that could use Tupac's talent. Tupac's signing to Death Row solidified its place in rap history both musically and financially.

The financial windfall that Death Row experienced was to the gain of everyone but Tupac. After his death, records showed Tupac had earned little

Tupac with Treach from Naughty by Nature at the "Hip-Hop Hooray" video shoot on December 5, 1992.
(Chi Modu/diverseimages/Getty Images)

Tupac with actress, producer, and director Rosie Perez at the 7th Annual Soul Train Music Awards in 1993.

(Ron Galella/WireImage.com)

Rapper/actor Tupac Shakur with his mother Afeni Shakur, in the courthouse hallway after his arrest on sodomy charges involving a twenty-year-old woman at the Hotel Parker Meridien.

(Kimberly Butler/Time Life Pictures/Getty Images)

Entrance to the Hotel Parker Meridien where Tupac Shakur was staying during the alleged sodomy incident.

(Kimberly Butler/Time Life Pictures/Getty Images)

Tupac leaving the courthouse after he was found guilty of sodomy. The day before he had been shot five times in the lobby of a recording studio.

(© James Leynse/Corbis)

Tupac had a short but intense affair with Tiffany Davis in 1996. She had a reputation for dating some of the most powerful and richest men in the music industry and on the streets.

(Courtesy of Toi Davis)

Snoop Dogg and Tupac at the 1996 MTV Video Music Awards. Nine days later, Tupac would be dead. (Ron Galella/WireImage.com)

Writer and rap artist Sister Souljah speaks with the press while attending the 1996 Hip-Hop Day of Atonement in Manhattan. The event, sponsored by the Nation of Islam in response to the drive-by shooting of rapper Tupac Shakur, called for the end of the violence between the East Coast and the West Coast rap-music industry, and for hip-hop artists to become more responsible for their lyrics.

(© James Leynes/CORBIS)

Sean "P. Diddy" Combs, Naughty by Nature, and Run DMC and crew, paying tribute to Tupac Shakur at MTV20: Live and Almost Legal-Show.
(Kevin Kane/WireImage.com)

Afeni Shakur at an event following the world premiere of the documentary *Tupac Resurrection* in 2003.

(Lee Celano/WireImage.com)

Nas performs on stage wearing a Tupac Shakur T-shirt at the VH1 Hip-Hop Honors, October 3, 2004, in New York City. (Frank Micelotta/Getty Images)

Mopreme Shakur, Tupac's brother, in 2004.
(Maury Phillips/WireImage.com)

Tupac in 1994 at an evening celebrating actor Mickey
Rourke at Nello's.
(© Schwartzwald Lawrence/CORBIS SYGMA)

Tupac at the 1st Annual Minority Motion Pictures Awards in 1993. (Ron Galella/WireImage.com)

Tupac at the *Poetic Justice* premiere, 1993. (Ron Galella/WireImage.com)

In 1993 a defiant Tupac makes his feelings known as he
walks past a court officer.
(Kimberly Butler/Time Life Pictures/Getty Images)

Tupac at the 1994 Benefit Auction For Intercambios Culturales Project For El Salvador.
(Ron Galella/WireImage.com)

Tupac in 1995 at the 10th Annual Soul Train Music Awards.
(Steve Granitz Archive/WireImage.com)

Tupac in 1994 at the premiere of *I Like It Like That* to benefit Women In Need.
(Ron Galella/WireImages.com)

Tupac Shakur.
(Time Life Pictures/DMI/Time Life Pictures/Getty Images)

from his jail-cell deal with Suge. When Tupac died, he had only about $100,000 in his bank account. The house he thought was his in Woodland Hills was rented; his cars were leased, and his music was controlled by Suge. That was all until Afeni Shakur filed a racketeering lawsuit against Death Row, Suge Knight, and David Kenner. In her suit, she alleged that the group had conspired to steal from Tupac. The suit charged Kenner with malpractice and breach of fiduciary duty, claiming that his "purported representation of Tupac was in hopeless conflict" with his own interests since Kenner was both an attorney for Death Row and an owner of it. After failing to get a response, Afeni sought to block the release of Tupac's next album. Connie Bruck of the *New Yorker* reported that "Jimmy Iovine met with Afeni and her lawyer, Richard Fischbein, and agreed that Interscope would pay her an immediate $3 million with more to come. And it was Interscope, not Death Row, which underwrote a memorial service for Tupac in Atlanta in November. Interscope has, in a way, been a model of corporate responsibility. Indeed, in a strictly corporate sense it has done more than was required. Tupac was not officially Interscope's artist, after all. But Interscope executives may feel a level of responsibility for having pushed Tupac into Suge's arms."

Interscope stood to win only if they signed a deal with Afeni because they would still be distributing the successful Tupac catalog that Afeni would control. Afeni Shakur successfully litigated her case with

Suge Knight and Death Row Records with the help of lawyer Donald David and had Tupac's intellectual properties reverted to the estate. Suge still had control over two albums that he owned, which are now distributed by Koch Records, so he gets royalties from these as well as other albums on Interscope.

This was just the beginning for Afeni Shakur's David and Goliath–like battle. The first lawsuit filed against the estate of Tupac Shakur was from his thought-to-be father Billy Garland, who now was asking for his just due of 50 percent of his son's entire earnings. A judge dismissed the case, saying that Garland gave less than $500 and a bag of peanuts to his son. The case was then settled for an estimated $890,000, which some people point to as proof of Garland being Tupac's biological father. His was only to be the beginning of a string of civil suits against the estate.

With this knowledge, Tupac's mother armed herself with a team of accountants, lawyers, and business managers and set upon reorganizing her son's estate. One of her top priorities was paying all of the musicians, singers, engineers, and producers who were caught in the middle of Death Row's scheme and the various lawsuits. Afeni Shakur told Jasmine Guy in her autobiography, *Afeni Shakur: Evolution of a Revolutionary,* that Deloitte and Touche, the auditors who combed through the Death Row and Interscope records, were located in the World Trade Center on September 11, 2001, when the towers came down, and they had to leave the building.

"They panicked and ran out of their offices," Afeni says. "And then they remembered they had left Tupac's stuff on the desk . . . Jasmine, they went back and got this shit! Then they left the building. God is such a good God. He works in all of these ways and places."

In all, Afeni had to find her way through a legal maze. Dina LaPolt told PR.com that "when Tupac died, he never had a music lawyer. When you are a recording artist every royalty payment that goes to producers and other third party royalty participants, people that perform on your album, comes out of the artist's royalty. And if they write music with the artist, then the artist has to do agreements with them, like song split agreements, so these people share in the publishing money. When Tupac died, nothing was papered on his behalf. Under the terms of his recording agreement, they were allowed to release all of his albums notwithstanding the fact that none of the paperwork was done, and they just didn't pay him. They just froze all the royalty streams and kept their profits. When I got involved, there was literally over $13 million in frozen royalty payments that belonged to Tupac, his producers, all his co-writers. It was just awful. Me, in connection with another lawyer, Donald David, who was very influential in getting this untangled as well, and then the lawyer for our publishing company, Robert Allen, we literally . . . two and half years of our lives we just went song by song and worked all of the copyrights split. Tupac didn't have agreements with his producers so nobody was getting paid. All the songwriters who wrote songs with Tupac, whether it was Dr. Dre or the Outlawz or whoever, none of them were getting their songwriter royalties."

Interscope Records has been widely regarded as the most successful new label since Geffen Records, and its success cannot be attributed solely to its affiliation with Death Row. Interscope has hugely successful rock groups and the legacy of Death Row Records reads like a roster of blockbuster sales. Is gangsta rap, with its scandal, controversy, and loss of lives, profitable? The recent sale of shares of Interscope to Universal for more than $300 million answers the question. Suge Knight hasn't fared as well. In spring of 2006, Marion "Suge" Knight and his Death Row Records filed for bankruptcy, just hours before the rap mogul was expected to lose control of his label in a $107 million civil court judgment. By seeking bankruptcy protection, Knight forestalled a court order that would have handed control of the label to a special court officer known as a receiver. Superior Court judge Ronald Sohigian issued the order after finding that Knight had failed to make good on the $107 million judgment obtained the previous March by Lydia Harris, who claimed he cheated her out of a 50 percent stake in Death Row. Suge Knight's problems with the law have continued over the years. Two years after his 2001 release, Knight spent an additional ten months in prison for violating his parole for allegedly striking a Hollywood nightclub valet. In 2005, the

Associated Press reported that "Suge Knight was shot and wounded in Miami while attending a party that coincided with the MTV awards for the Grammy-winning blockbuster-selling artist Kanye West."

Still, Knight continues to try to profit off Tupac. Beaux Carson of Carson Signature Films inked a deal with Knight to tell his version of the events that unfolded surrounding the shooting of Tupac. Carson described the film as *"Training Day* meets *The Godfather."*

What is the price for Death Row's gangsterism, or Tupac's passion to bring a new order of social change? Maybe it is said best in the book by Niccolò Machiavelli, *The Prince:* "We must bear in mind, then, that there is nothing more difficult and dangerous, or more doubtful of success, than an attempt to introduce a new order of things in any state. For the innovator has for enemies all those who derived advantages from the old order of things while those who expect to be benefited by the new institutions will be but lukewarm defenders."

NINE
Blasphemy

I'm contemplating plots; wondering which door to go; brotha getting shot; coming back resurrected
— TUPAC SHAKUR

Lyrics like the ones above from the cut "Blasphemy" on *Makaveli* have many speculating whether Tupac actually died on September 13, 1996. Many theories have been tossed around since Tupac was shot. Some are almost plausible, while others force our imaginations to reach a little beyond the edge of reason.

One thing is undeniable: Tupac is alive through the legacy he left behind in his music. He also touches people's lives daily through the Tupac Amaru Shakur Foundation, which his mother, Afeni, founded in 1997. The mission of the foundation is to provide training and support for students who aspire to enhance their creative talents. Tupac believed that everyone should be judged by his or her character and given an opportunity to become a better person. What better way to represent him and his work than by empowering children to express themselves creatively? The foundation encourages freedom of expression, serves as a resource for families, and empowers through education.

Afeni formed the foundation as a way to bring quality arts training to young people. A broad range of training is offered at the Annual Performing Arts Day Camp held at the Tupac Amaru Shakur Center for the Arts in Georgia. Disciplines include creative writing, vocal technique, acting, stage set design, dance, poetry and spoken word, and the business of entertainment. The foundation has also hosted essay competitions throughout the United States, charity golf tournaments, and awarded scholarships to students pursuing undergraduate degrees.

Since 1999, TASF's annual Performing Arts Camps (PAC) have provided quality training and support for youth who aspire to enhance their creative talents. Classes have included acting, creative writing, dance, vocal training, set and stage design, business of entertainment, and video production. To date, more than three hundred youths ages twelve to eighteen have participated in this annual summer camp. The skills acquired from the intense four-week training period culminates in a closing ceremony production. Unlike Tupac's experience with the Baltimore School for the Arts, auditions are not required of their students. PACamps serve as a means for students to explore the possibilities offered by the arts and entertainment industries and discover unknown talents hidden within themselves. By providing individual attention to each participant, they help students gain an understanding of peer leadership, performance skills, and theatrical production.

TASF's instructors are world-renowned artists and industry professionals whose commitment to the foundation's mission is clearly demonstrated by the students' performances during the closing ceremony production. For more information contact:

Tupac Amaru Shakur Center for the Arts
5616 Memorial Drive
Stone Mountain, GA 30083
404-298-4222

The importance of Tupac's legacy should outweigh the innuendo and rumors that abound, but as with any untimely and tragic death, it's easier to cope by making assumptions about what happened, or to question whether it even happened at all. No one except his killer knows exactly why Tupac's life came to a tragic end, but there are many theories and rumors out there.

There are theories surrounding Tupac's death on September 13, 1996. The first is that Orlando Anderson, a rumored member of the Crips, was retaliating for the earlier beating he took at the MGM Grand Hotel.

Three months earlier, in a Southern California mall near Long Beach, three members of The Mob Piru Bloods went into a Foot Locker to purchase some shoes. One of the Bloods worked for Death Row Records and was wearing the diamond-cut medallion that was worn by Death Row staff and artists. When they left the mall, the Bloods were confronted by a group of Crips and the Death Row medallion was stolen.

On September 7, 1996, as Tupac was leaving the Mike Tyson fight at the MGM Grand with his boys from Death Row, he was pulled to the side by the Blood whose chain had been stolen, who pointed out someone in the lobby as the guy who stole his chain. This person was Orlando Anderson, who looked eerily like Tupac. Tupac immediately headed over to confront Orlando and a fight broke out. Tupac and the Death Row entourage viciously beat Orlando and left before the cops arrived.

Here's where fact breaks into theory. Orlando spoke with the police who arrived on the scene, then he left the hotel. He may have left to tell his boys, who belonged to the Southside Crips, what happened and to get revenge for the attack. From there you can fill in the blanks. It wouldn't have been hard to find the Death Row entourage, because Suge owned Club 662 in Las Vegas and there was to be an after-party for the fight there that night.

A couple of weeks after Tupac's murder, Metro Police arrested Orlando Anderson. Anderson's family released a statement denying he was connected to Shakur's killing in Las Vegas: "Tupac Shakur, the talented musical genius, fell at the hands of a violent cruel drive-by shooter or shooters in Las Vegas. That's a fact. That person, however, is not Orlando." Orlando was released due to lack of evidence. He maintained his innocence up until May 29, 1998, the day he was murdered at a Los Angeles car wash.

The second theory of Tupac's death is a little more sinister in nature and involves people he trusted. Many believe that Suge Knight was directly involved in the murder of Tupac, and even that of his friend-turned-nemesis Biggie Smalls. The theory begins September 16, 1995, when Tupac signed with Death Row Records.

Tupac lacked the resources he needed to get out of prison. Not knowing who else to turn to, he contacted Suge Knight at Death Row Records. Suge agreed to arrange for Tupac's bail and to secure the bond; in exchange, Tupac would finally sign a multi-album deal with Death Row. In Tupac's view, he was choosing the lesser of two evils. His deal basically gave Suge and Death Row lawyer David Kenner the right to represent him in all his musical and criminal issues. When Tupac got out of prison he was flown straight to California and started to fulfill his contractual obligations to Death Row.

The first Death Row album for Tupac, *All Eyez on Me,* was a double CD, which covered the first two albums of the three-album contract. Everything wasn't always what it seemed publicly with Death Row Records. While Tupac tried to give the impression of a united front at the label, things were falling apart and he wanted out. The night Tupac was shot, things occurred that were out of the ordinary for Tupac and over which Suge had an enormous amount of control.

In addition, it was rumored that Suge and David Kenner were embezzling money from Tupac's account right under his nose. Tupac was being charged for items totaling hundreds of thousands of dollars that had nothing to do with his contract, including rent on other people's apartments, car repairs and purchases for others, and excessive video and audio production costs that in many instances weren't even for his projects.

A 1997 *Vanity Fair* article claimed that Tupac was planning to leave Death Row and had even gone as far as contacting Warner Bros. about a new deal. The piece asserted that Tupac wanted to settle down with Kidada Jones and lead a much calmer and drama-free lifestyle. For these reasons, many speculate that Suge got word of Tupac's intentions and arranged to have him killed so he could maintain, control, and reap the financial rewards of Tupac's musical library. If you listen closely to the first three seconds of *The Don Killuminati: The 7 Day Theory* by Makaveli, the new name Tupac took, it is said by some that you can hear "Suge shot me." Others say it is "Shouldn't have shot him." If the former is true, it's not known how this got on the track, but it has been said that Tupac's friend and a member of the Outlawz, Yafeu Fula, added it. Coincidentally, Yafeu was killed a month to the day after Tupac died. He was shot once in the head and killed in what police say was a drug-related incident in the hallway of his girlfriend's housing project in Orange, New Jersey.

According to this particular theory, it is speculated that Suge had Biggie killed in almost the same manner as Tupac only nine months later to make it seem as if Biggie had Tupac killed. After a Soul Train Music Awards party in Los Angeles, Biggie was shot five times while sitting in the passenger seat of a Suburban. There are just as many rumors surrounding Biggie's death as there are surrounding Tupac's. Both murders remain unsolved. Which leads into the next widely speculated theory: Biggie had Tupac killed.

In 2002, a reporter for the *Los Angeles Times*, Chuck Phillips, claimed that after speaking with several Crip gang members it became apparent that Biggie was involved in Tupac's murder. Phillips, through information gathered from his sources, claimed that Biggie was in Las Vegas September 7, 1996, and met with Crips who told him about Tupac's fight with Orlando Anderson. Claiming this was the perfect cover for a hit, they asked for $1 million in exchange for Tupac's death and were given Biggie's very own 9-millimeter Glock to do the job. Phillips asserted that Biggie had maintained connections with the Crips in the past. He hired them as bodyguards, got them into music-related parties and functions, and even brought them onstage during concerts. Biggie always maintained his innocence and lack of involvement in Tupac's death. When he died nine months later in the very same way Tupac was killed, his family continued to maintain his innocence. Biggie's mother, Voletta Wallace, and friends supplied evidence to refute Phillips's allegations. They supplied documentation to MTV after the Phillips article ran showing that Biggie had reserved studio time the night of September 7, 1996, in a New York recording studio coincidentally owned by Puffy. They also provided date-stamped digital audiotapes for that night's session that went well into the morning of September 8. His manager and Lil' Cease also vouched for Biggie's whereabouts that night, stating they were both with him in New York.

The last theory deals with the FBI and police targeting Tupac and setting him up. It was widely known that Tupac had bumped heads with law enforcement officers across the country and even had a file with the Federal Bureau of Investigation with Eazy-E for extortion. Given his numerous physical altercations with law enforcement agents, whom Tupac considered the biggest gang in America, he wasn't winning favor with them. The whole theory of police involvement goes back to Tupac's first shooting, in 1994. Tupac asserted two things that stemmed from that shooting: first, that former associate Jacques Agnant was a police informant who set him up; and second, that he saw police officers on the scene during the shooting who did nothing.

In the Las Vegas shooting there were several instances of police misconduct, at the least total nonchalance and disregard for the shooting and proper procedure and protocol. First, the officers who arrived on the scene never secured it. The two Las Vegas bicycle officers who had stopped Suge minutes before for a noise ordinance issue heard the shots and failed to pursue the white Cadillac and secure the scene for evidence purposes and gathering witnesses. From all accounts there were at least three other cars in the immediate vicinity on this major strip, as well as bystanders on foot.

The Las Vegas Police also claimed that there was no lack of witnesses to the murder. Yafeu Fula even told the police he thought he could identify the shooter, as he was in a car immediately following the BMW 750i in which Suge and Tupac were traveling that night. But they failed to question Yafeu or get a description of the shooter to give to the public for identification, and shortly thereafter Yafeu was killed. Even the Los Angeles Police Department criticized the Las Vegas PD for their shoddy job on the Tupac murder case.

Finally, there was an investigation into how the award-winning *Las Vegas Sun* police reporter Cathy Scott got an autopsy photo of Tupac. The gruesome photo was exclusively printed in her book *The Killing of Tupac Shakur*, but of course its release to a layperson outside of the coroner's office is illegal. There was a formal investigation into how and who leaked this photo to a member of the press, but no conclusions were drawn at the end of the investigation.

The autopsy photo leads to the second group of theories surrounding Tupac's shooting. There are many people who believe Tupac is still alive and hiding out in wait to make a grand return. Some of these theories are based on mere coincidence and timing, while others are based on Tupac's own words, and still more are based on conjecture and innuendo from those who cannot accept Tupac's death. Here are some of the songs that skeptics have pointed to as evidence that Tupac is still alive:

"Ain't Hard 2 Find"
"Ain't Mad at Cha & Toss Em Up"
"Ambitionz az a Ridah"
"Blashemy"
"Fuckin' with the Wrong Nigga"
"Good Life"
"Hail Mary"
"Hold Ya Head"
"Krazy"
"Life of an Outlaw"
"Lost Souls"
"Made Niggaz"
"My Closest Road Dawgs"
"Never Had a Friend Like Me"
"Niggaz Done Changed"
"Smile"
"Staring Through My Rearview"
"Thug Luv"
"Thugs Cry"(with Bizzy Bone of Bone Thugs and Harmony)
"Troublesome 96"
"Unconditional Love"
"What's Next"
"When We Ride on Our Enemies"
"White Man's World"
"WorldWide Mob Figgaz"

The various lyrics can be found on the websites www.hitemup.com and www.thugzarmy.com. Of course, what weakens this theory is the fact that Tupac always spoke about death in his music.

The numerology theories are intriguing. An examination of Tupac's writing shows that he used numbers as a shorthand form of writing. Many fans became fascinated with the numbers theory because of a string of coincidences focusing on the number 7. The title of the first album by Makaveli a.k.a. Tupac was *The 7 Day Theory*. Tupac was shot on September 7 and survived for seven days, leading fans to believe *The 7 Day Theory* was a message that Tupac was alive. Tupac's album *All Eyez on Me* was released on Febuary 13, 1996. Tupac died on September 13, 1996, making the album's release date exactly seven months after his death. He officially died at 4:03 P.M. 4+0+3 = 7. Tupac also died at the age of twenty-five, and 2+5 = 7.

TEN

How Long Will They Mourn Me?

Damn, why they take another soldier
— TUPAC SHAKUR

Tupac's haunting similarities with the character he played so convincingly in the movie *Juice* shadows his own tragedy. The obsession with keeping it real, his insecurities, or the demons that were never overcome eventually led to the demise and death of Tupac Shakur.

At Tupac's memorial service at the House of The Lord Church in Brooklyn, New York—the church Tupac, his mother, and sister joined when he was ten—the Reverend Herbert Daughtry, a well-respected civil rights advocate, asked the question, "Who will weep for Tupac Shakur?" In a booming voice wrought with emotion, he shouted, "I will!" Reverend Daughtry was memorializing someone he loved as a son. He acknowledged Tupac's ambition to fight against the injustice suffered by African Americans and the disenfranchised around the world, and compared Tupac to Martin Luther King, Jr., and Malcolm X.

Tupac enjoyed the support of several prominent black leaders, including the Reverend Daughtry, the Reverend Jesse Jackson, and the Reverend Al Sharpton, who supported him while he was in prison and visited him at the prison hospital. "Sometimes the lure of violent culture is so magnetic that even when one overcomes it with material success, it continues to call. Tupac just couldn't break the cycle," the Reverend Jesse Jackson said.

"Tupac was a young man of turmoil. He had forces within him. Tupac had an artistic force, a revolution force, and a drive for social change, particularly for people of African ancestry caught in the vortex of turmoil," said Reverend Daughtry.

"To lose a young man like Tupac Shakur with brilliance and talent, at twenty-five years old, is indicative of what black males in this society are facing. We are not living long enough to realize our full potential. Malcolm X, in his young years, was a gangbanger, a drug dealer. Tupac would have evolved naturally, but black men are dying before they get their chance to grow," said Minister Conrad Muhammad. How did a twenty-five-year-old man named after an Inca warrior, who was raised to be a Black Prince by two Black Panthers, become the most controversial rapper and actor, and most of all the most influential revolutionary of our time?

This question has been explored in classrooms in some of the top learning institutions in the country. Recently, Michael Eric Dyson, author of *Holler If You Hear Me: Searching for Tupac Shakur,* led a conference about Tupac at Harvard University. He argues that "Tupac is a martyr who should never be forgotten. Tupac is, by virtue of his unparalleled problems, the perfect embodiment of his generation's genius and grief. He is the perfect symbol of the moral aspirations of what may be termed the hip-hop generation and the contradictions that it faces as well. He lives on in our memories and in our hearts."

The Harvard conference explored how Tupac became a folk hero, almost saintlike. He inspired so many different types of youth, despite his unpredictable and often erratic behavior still offering hope. The hope that Tupac Shakur instilled is now translated into a political tool.

The *Los Angeles Times* reported that perhaps "Tupac took lessons from the Last Poets and Public Enemy." "Tupac laced his music with political messages," stated Crispin Sartwell, a teacher of political science at Dickinson College in California. "If Thomas Paine or Karl Marx were here today, they would be issuing records rather than pamphlets."

Not everyone agrees. John McWhorter, of the conservative Manhattan Institute, argues "that this so-called conscious rap as some have termed it is just gangtsa rap in another form. It is barking about another subject from street violence, women, and guns to politics and ignores the fact that a whole new class of middle-class black Americans has emerged without stopping to berate or lash out at anyone." He says it is ultimately all about spitting in the eye of the powers that be. "But that is precisely what the millions of blacks who are making the best of themselves in modern America have done. Contrary to what we are often led to believe, spitting is not serious activism. It's merely attitude."

Attitude is the least of our worries. Russell Simmons and the Hip-Hop Summit rallied thousands of young people to oppose budget cuts in New York City schools. Shortly thereafter, Mayor Bloomberg changed his mind about the issue. Tupac's inspiration was felt when Kanye West vented his anger on a telethon about the Katrina victims.

Macy Gray, who recently teamed up with Afeni Shakur to provide residences for displaced Hurricane Katrina families near Shakur's home in Stone Mountain, Georgia, told MTV: "Me, and some friends of mine, we're going to adopt ten families. We're taking them to this apartment building [in Atlanta] where we got them ten units." Gray also helped the parents get jobs and get their kids registered for school. She said, "Tupac inspired all musicians not only to look within ourselves but to look to how we could be instrumental in helping other people. I know that if Tupac was alive he would have gone ballistic about this Katrina shit. He lived with his heart on his sleeve and knew what it was like to have nothing. We miss you Pac, and his legacy lives in all of us."

Ebony magazine reports, "Poet Giovanni says she never met Tupac, but recognizes his importance. 'Tupac is right there with Malcolm X and Emmett Till; he is an image of possibility who was cut down,' Giovanni says. 'I will do more for him.' Such strong convictions, coupled with the marvels of modern technology that literally allow deceased artists to continue to pump out hit recordings and stellar performances, will work to further cement the stars' immortality for generations. Because of this, Tupac really does live.

"The phenomenal posthumous staying power of Tupac and the Notorious B.I.G. continues to spark national debate about their significance in the world. 'Biggie only put out two albums, but in ten years he will still be remembered because he molded a foundation for a whole new generation for hip-hop,' says Jake Brown, author of *King of New York: The Life and Times of the Notorious B.I.G.*"

Technology has played a hand in allowing mourners to grieve with one another across the world. The Internet and twenty-four-hour news channels also feed the rumor mill concerning a celebrity's demise. As a result, sociologists explain that the untimely death of a celebrity is generally followed by a modern-day communal mourning ritual. There was no public funeral service for Tupac Shakur—adding to the growing conspiracy theory of many fans that he is indeed still alive—but his legion of fans all around the globe still found deep and meaningful ways to show their love.

Music journalist Big Ced agrees: "I was not there nor anywhere in the vicinity, but I personally have always believed that Tupac is still alive. The reports we were getting was that after he was shot that he had an 80 percent chance for living; he was in a coma. Then he died and was cremated. There was no funeral service and the memorial service was abruptly canceled. Tupac was already larger than life. People, his fans, would like to mourn him, pay their last respect. The way it went down was so mysterious. He was one of the biggest hip-hop artists. How can all of this happen within days?" The Black Panthers are good at hiding people. Then his album is named after Machiavelli, a man who faked his death; it is too coincidental.

"Tupac was just so talented and rapped from the soul. He made you believe what he said, he made you feel, if he was having fun you know, if it was serious, you knew it. Most artists just front for the camera. But Tupac is our modern-day Marvin Gaye, a Sam Cooke.

A tortured soul." The world indeed lost a black prince who was ahead of his time.

Some artists begged fans not to mourn for Tupac. Shock G/Money-B of Digital Underground, who understood Tupac and his mission, said, "If you want to mourn, do it for your own personal loss. Don't mourn for 'Pac, remember him for his art and don't be sad for his death. 'Pac lived a short, fast, concentrated, an intense life. He lived a seventy-year life in twenty-five years. He went out the way he wanted: in the glitter of the fast life, hit record on the charts, new movie in the can, and money in the pocket. All 'Pac wanted was to hear himself on the radio and see himself on the movie screen. He did all that—and more."

Personal friends reflected on Tupac's love and friendship. Bookeem Woodbine said, "He was passionate about his craft, and he never brought his persona to the table. It was just Tupac, a soul who cared so much about the world and his friends. None of us can even begin to comprehend the talent and vision that he had, it was beyond our grasp. I felt he was prophetic and that shows even in the concept of our last video together 'I Ain't Mad at Cha.' I still personally have a hard time dealing with the parallels of how his life ended in comparison to the video. I said this ten years ago and it still rings true, that in years to come music and cinema of today will be considered a renaissance era of sorts and I think Tupac was on the forefront of a lot of that. People will look back and say that Tupac was a true renaissance magician."

Others explained his place in history. Chuck D of Public Enemy said, "To me Tupac is like the James Dean of our times. Basically, a rebel without a cause.

And the industry and the media are partially responsible for whatever goes down: in accenting the negative aspects of a black celebrity. It's the soup-up, gas-up treatment. They soup him up, they're not there on the downside. People think that this man's life was entertainment. One of our best talents is gone over some bullshit. I'm fuckin' pissed. I ain't putting up tears. Tears ain't gonna do a damn thing. Interscope will go on to sell ten million copies of this album. Make a scholarship fund out of their share of the money. That's what I call making things happen."

Treach of Naughty By Nature ran with Tupac and loved him like a brother. He said, "My man 'Pac, he didn't have a criminal record until he made a record. Once you get into the light, a lot of stuff comes on to you. One thing I can say, he was one of the realest niggas that lived. He said whatever was on his mind; he never bit his tongue for nuthin'."

"When I heard that Pac died, I was in studio session in Greensboro, North Carolina. I had just come back from getting something to eat and the guys were outside the studio saying that Pac died. I was in a state of shock," Big Daddy Kane recalls. "What I admired about him most was his determination. When he wanted to achieve something, whether it was rapping or acting, he went after it. A lot of people just dream; Pac chased his dream and made it come true. I remember when Tupac, the rapper Eric B, Hammer, Suge, and I checked out the Mike Tyson vs. Frank Bruno fight in Vegas. We hung out for two days before the fight, kickin' it and remembering old times. I just casually said to Pac, let's record a joint together and Suge and Pac said shit, let's do it tonight. Pac and I flew back to L.A. from Vegas and recorded the song 'Wherever You Are,' which eventually was released on the *Makaveli* lost tapes. What fascinated me about working in the studio with him was his drive. Tupac knocked out our song and three others and recorded them; he also wrote a song for a beat that DJ Quick had put together and told the engineer that Quick needed to come up with something better."

Kane continues, "Normally cats go in a studio and do a song in one day. Tupac was a workaholic plus. With everything going, with Tupac's court cases, all of the arrests, a lot of people saw him as a troublemaker. I always thought he was a string radical brother who fought for what he believed in. He was never fighting to prove he was a thug, he fought for what he believed in with a sincere heart, more or less do not let anyone push you around."

Although Mobb Deep and Tupac stirred up controversy and sparred in song, it did not stop the members of the group from Havoc Mobb Deep. "I loved him before the confrontation; I loved him, and I loved his music. We was planning to see him but we didn't even get the chance. It's sad, man. I think the streets killed him. It wasn't no East Coast/West Coast thing, it was the streets. I think it was his mouth that killed him." Prodigy, also a member of the group Mobb Deep, echoed the same sentiments: "Between my crew and people over there on the West Coast, it's sad to see where it's going. I don't know how this started, but we need to get together. Once everybody can calm down, relax, and put our troubles behind us, we can strive for a better tomorrow.

"Tupac will be mourned because he related well to

the community as a whole. He showed so much heart as a person, sometimes as an activist, that it was hard not to notice, he was a very emotional and mysterious person and he was a Gemini like myself."

"I miss working with Tupac, I miss him dropping by the studio. It is a weird feeling to expect to hear from somebody and you don't hear from them. I kept in touch with Mopreme and it helped fill a void. A lot of people go by what they see, everyone does not know Tupac more than a good friend, he was real true friend, he was one of the realest people I ever knew," said music producer DMAQ.

Sy Smith, singer and songwriter: "Tupac is still mourned because he lived his life in front of the world —unafraid to show his mistakes, his sorrows, his pain, and his joy. Even though he was considered by some to be a misogynistic gangsta rapper, he actually showed people that he was multidimensional. Tupac honored women, he was proud of his heritage, his cities, his culture and he inspired a movement that was embarking on all of these values. When we lost Tupac, we lost a movement that was on the verge of being very powerful. I remember the summer that 'I Get Around' came out and my cousin and I drove to Jones Beach in New York and listened to it on a CASS-SINGLE!!! All the way to the beach! We had so much fun listening to that song . . . Every time I hear it, I think about that day at Jones Beach. I think Pac inspired other rappers to show different sides of themselves . . . Most rappers were hesitant to say anything political or positive in their songs (unless they were sociopolitical artists to begin with). Tupac showed artists that it's important to express more than one aspect of life in artistry."

Tupac's loss was internationally felt.

Bay-C from the Reggae Group TKO said, "Our music has been influenced tremendously by the hip-hop of the '90s. We were watching Tupac when he was with Digital Underground. We believed in his desire to have positive and not negative images of black people, we understood his Thug Life Code and felt his passion for music. Tupac is mourned because of the tragic way in which he passed, he was young and had so much potential. When it comes down to it, Tupac may have lost his life because of music and how ugly it can get. But Pac's legacy still lives on in his music; he left musical footprints."

The same sentiment is echoed in fellow group TKO member Craig T: "Tupac inspired me through his music, it was an expression and an extension of his life. His music is now immortal. If you look at the clips of Tupac most of them are in defiance of law and authority and he was able to say what he felt. Most people wish they could be that free. In my country of Jamaica, Tupac is revered and will always be considered a fallen soldier. He stood for what he believed and in our eyes he died with honor."

Bingo Kenoly, a hugely successful international Christian rap artist, has been named as one of an increasing number of Christian artists who are rescuing hip-hop and rap from its preoccupation with drugs and drive-by shootings. He said, "There is a fine line between addressing the facts of your environment or your frustration about your situation and presenting your violent thoughts as a solution. Tupac never made a clear distinction between the two.

"Tupac's music has reference to God and speared the

message of forgiveness and a desire to have a closer relationship with God in songs such as 'Blasphemy' and 'Hail Mary.' It is also obvious to anyone who actually took time to listen to Pac's music that he was looking for God. It's very clear that he wanted a relationship with God, but I think the reason why that was hard to see at times is because he was a victim of his environment. If you hang around nothing but gang bangers, drug dealers, and thugs, that is all that you will portray. However, Tupac and I do share some similar views."

Bingo continues, "We both are very vocal about what we represent. Regardless of what people might think about it. We are both very passionate about our beliefs and standing by them no matter what. I love the fact that he was not scared to say what was on his mind. He didn't sugarcoat anything. He said what he meant and meant what he said. Whether you could swallow it or not was your problem. And he remained true to himself even when it was not popular to do so.

"Tupac is mourned and will always be mourned because he had a rare ability to connect with the audience in a way that had never been seen before. His delivery of every lyric of every song he presented was unprecedented. It didn't matter what he was talking about. You felt him. If he was mad you felt his anger. If he was sad you felt his pain. Whatever he was going through on that particular song, he took you through that experience with him. And that's why he will be forever mourned. In a world where you try to insulate yourself from feeling any emotion to prevent from being hurt, Tupac made us feel."

C. Delores Tucker, a rival of Tupac, utilized his death to frame her mission, which she felt was misrepresented.

She says, "As I reflect upon the life and death of Tupac Shakur, I am reminded of the African proverb that tests us: 'It takes a whole village to raise a child.' Simple and eloquent in its message, it has a message for all of us—including the entertainment industry that molded and shaped the slain rapper and his music.

"Yes, the leaders of the entertainment industry village who produce and distribute the music known as gangsta rap are indeed responsible for the lives of its children, its gangsta rappers. And as the elders of that industry, it is their responsibility to provide guidance and leadership to the young rappers who aspire to the heights of their craft. But when those leaders fail to provide the moral grounding to their charges, they are nothing more than irresponsible adults. And anyone who forsakes his or her child in the quest for the almighty dollar is unworthy of anyone's respect. And as they abandon these youth in the pursuit of money, money, money—as they condone, support, and profit from this immoral music—they become conspirators of doom. One chief conspirator in this human tragedy is Interscope's Ted Field, an heir to the Marshall Field fortune. Field was quoted in a recent *Wall Street Journal* as saying 'you can tell the people who want to stop us from releasing controversial rap music one thing: kiss my a—.'

"Tupac, (Field's star pupil) expressed a similar attitude toward me when he immortalized me in several songs featured on his double disc CD, *All Eyez on Me*. 'C. Delores Tucker, you're a m—— f——, instead of trying to help a brother, you destroy a n——a' (from 'How Do You Want It') and 'Keep you head up and your legs closed Dear Ms. Delores Tucker' (from 'Wonda Why They Call B').

"He was very disrespectful and defaming in his reference to me. Little did he realize, I am only trying to save our young brothers, rather than hurt them. Had he had any idea of my concern and passion for them, those lyrics would have been quite different, I am sure."

Since the death of her son, Afeni Shakur has become a force to be reckoned with. In Atlanta, she created the Tupac Amaru Shakur Foundation, and in 1997 she founded Amaru Entertainment, Inc. Amaru has released seven posthumous albums featuring unreleased music and a spoken word album, a book, and a feature film, *Tupac: Resurrection.*

The steady cycle of rappers who become victims of their very own entourages—who are pseudo-gangs, taking up petty beefs and escalating them to tragic killings—still continues. Afeni weighs in: "[It's been] nearly ten years since everything between Tupac and Biggie (The Notorious B.I.G.) and rappers today are paying a lot of lip service to the lessons they learned from that tragedy, but how many of them are actually showing it in their actions? For T.I. and Lil' Flip to actually sit down together and actually talk about their issues, rather than automatically resorting to violence, is a wonderful lesson for the rest of the rap community and the young audience that looks up to them."

Afeni recently launched her "Keep Kids Alive" campaign, designed to stop the unnecessary deaths that take the lives of one youth every eighteen minutes in the United States, through car accidents, suicides, and homicides. Of T.I. and Lil' Flip she says, "There are so many other ways to resolve conflicts than violence and the actions of these two young men are beautiful and mature responses to what could have escalated to something very tragic. This is precisely the type of example the rap community needs to be reminded of today before we have any more misfortunes on our hands that will forever affect so many lives. It will be a better world for all of us—especially the young people that idolize these artists. It was the world my son strived for and it is wonderful to see it actually having taken place in this instance. My hope is that others will see this, take it to heart, and truly learn from it."

It seems that Ms. Shakur has her work cut out for her. On the heels of the above-mentioned negotiation between rival rappers, Proof, rapper and confidant to Eminem, died in a hail of gunfire at a Detroit nightclub. In a separate incident Philant Johnson, 26, best friend and personal assistant to T.I., was killed in a shoot-out after a performance at a Cincinnati nightclub on I-75. Cynthia Tucker of *The Atlanta Journal-Consitution* reports that a couple of days earlier, Houston rapper Big Hawk was gunned down in his hometown. (His brother, rapper Fat Pat, was shot dead in 1998.) Those deaths followed a February shooting in New York that took the life of a bodyguard for rap star Busta Rhymes and a two-month killing spree in Las Vegas that left four rappers dead. On February 1, a Las Vegas police officer was shot and killed by aspiring rapper Amir Crump, who was also killed in the shoot-out with police.

No arrests have been made in several of the cases. Indeed, if history is any guide, many of the cases won't be solved. *Boston Globe* writer Renee Graham pointed out last year that the 1997 drive-by shooting of megastar Biggie Smalls, also known as the Notorious B.I.G., in Los Angeles, and the 1996 drive-by shooting of Tupac

Shakur, in Las Vegas, remain unsolved, as does the 2002 slaying of Jam Master Jay in New York. As Graham notes, "rap culture disrespects those who cooperate with the police, so law enforcement authorities have been unsuccessful in their efforts to uncover evidence that would stand up in court. (Rap artist Li'l Kim is serving a year in prison on a perjury charge, stemming from her lies about a shootout involving her entourage and another rap crew.) If the friends and associates of the slain rappers don't care enough to help the police find their killers, there is little hope for eventual justice. Besides, too many rappers, several of whom have criminal pasts, believe that violence only pumps up their street 'cred' (credibility) and fuels their popularity. At least the dead rappers get a big funeral and their heirs profit from increased sales. Millions of young black men across the country adopt them as role models and emulate their behavior. Some of them will die, too, but their deaths will be noted only by family and friends. It's no wonder that homicide remains a leading cause of death for young black men."

A Brooklyn rapper, MC Gravy, was shot in the buttock just before entering the Hot 97 radio station in New York City (notorious for several shootouts between rival rap groups). Gravy conducted his radio interview with the bullet still lodged in him, then went to the hospital. The New York City Police Department made a decision to install cameras that will be manned twenty-four hours a day and the radio station now has a new policy that includes no airplay by any artist who is involved in an altercation at the station. MC Gravy told MTV News, "I feel like, damn . . . Y'all stopping [airplay] on my end? Why me? Because I'm new? I'm just getting ready to do my thing. Y'all should have stopped [the violence] and had [surveillance] cameras [in front of the station]. I think [eventually] they gonna turn around and say, 'Man, we take that back. Gravy is a good guy. He's productive,' " MC said. "I take [the ban] as they don't know me. They're just protecting their jobs."

Gravy said he respects Hot 97 so much that immediately after the shooting, he hid the fact that he was hit and appeared on Flex's show (whose on air personality name is Funk Master Flex) as scheduled for a freestyle and interview. "What am I supposed to say? 'Flex, I can't do your show, even though it's my life. I just took a shot to the ass, I can't do it.' What does that sound like?" he said. "I had to do what I had to do. People are not seeing it that way. They're like, 'He's glorifying the shot.' N—a, I'm not glorifying the shot. I love my life more than rap. I'm not trying to take a shot for rap. I don't want to take no shot, brotha. Not in my thumb, my pinkie, nothing, brotha. Just imagine if I died. Would they play me then? They would play me because they would not want the world to assassinate their character. 'Here's a young man that was trying to do right and he got killed up there, and y'all not playing him?' "

Hip-hop artists are often tested for their street authenticity, skill set, and the realness of their autobiographical songs. But Tupac was different: He cared and had a message, and most of all he wanted to create change. In doing so he has developed a pop cultural phenomenon whose influence will be felt for at least our lifetime.

Tupac was able to take his forefathers' slogan of

Black Power and transform it into a modern-age global slogan for young people around the world who may have been born into situations beyond their control, such as poverty, hunger, homelessness, or abuse, showing them that they can rise above their circumstances regardless of where they are from. One can almost see him leading a chant, with his fist up in the air as he shouts, self-power, self-power!

Ilyasah Shabazz, daughter of Malcolm X and Dr. Betty Shabazz and author of *Growing Up X*, explained why we still mourn for Tupac as we have mourned for her father and mother: "You couldn't help but to admire and gravitate toward Tupac, this young brother who possessed great compassion, a brother who articulated the love, the pains, and the struggle of his self and his people. For such, Tupac Shakur will always be remembered. When I think of his struggle on behalf of humanity, the parallels to the life of my father come to mind."

Shabazz continues, "Tupac and Malcolm were both reared by activists whose commitment to peace and freedom underscored every lesson taught to their young children. The Shakurs in the Black Panther Party and the Littles in The Marcus Garvey Movement were students of history who understood the greatness of Africa and the later plight of Africans of the Diaspora. As parents, they were determined to right the wrongs of injustice and in the process instilled in their sons, young Tupac and young Malcolm, the core values of self-help, self-reliance, and a historically rich African identity. Both Tupac and Malcolm were emboldened by the courage of their parents to fight fearlessly in the struggle for human rights. As my father said and as

Tupac understood, 'A man who stands for nothing will fall for anything.' And as such, Tupac Shakur's life still echoes. . . . These young bold captains will never be forgotten as long as there are souls who hunger, thirst, and speak . . . for Truth."

Tupac Shakur's
Personal Reading List

The following books are just a small, varied sample of the books Tupac read. He was inspired by many authors from around the world and was able to analyze and apply the thoughts and philosophies of different writers whom he admired. His music spoke volumes and touched many.

1984
by George Orwell, 1st World Press

Ah, This!
by Bhagwan Shree Rajneesh

All God's Children: The Boskett Family and the American Tradition of Violence
by Fox Butterfield, Knopf Publishing Group

All You Need to Know About the Music Business
by Donald Passman, Simon & Schuster

And Still I Rise
by Maya Angelou, Random House Publishing Group

The Art of War
by Sun Tzu, Westview Press

Assata: An Autobiography
by Assata Shakur, Chicago Review Press, Inc.

At the Bottom of the River
by Jamaica Kincaid, Farrar, Straus and Giroux
 Publishers

The Autobiography of Malcolm X
by Malcolm X and Alex Haley, Random House
 Publishing Group

Bhagavad-Gita As It Is
by A. C. Bhaktive-danta Swami Prabhupada,
 Bhaktivedanta Book Trust

Black Like Me
by John Howard Griffin, Buccaneer Books, Inc.

*Black Sister: Poetry by Black American Women, 1746
 to 1980*
Edited by Earlene Stetson, Indiana University Press

Blues People
by LeRoi Jones (Imamu Amiri Baraka), Quill/William
 Morrow Publishers

The Catcher in the Rye
by J. D. Salinger, Little, Brown, & Company

Complete Illustrated Book of Psychic Sciences
by Walter B. Gibson and Litzka R. Gibson, Random
 House Publishing Group

The Confessions of Nat Turner
by William Styron, Knopf Publishing Group

The Destiny of Nations
by Alice A. Bailey, Lucis Publishing Company

The Diary of Anaïs Nin, Vol. 1
by Anaïs Nin and Gunther Stuhlmann, Harcourt

The Dictionary of Cultural Literacy: What Every American Needs to Know
by E. D. Hirsch, James Trefil, and Joseph F. Kett, Houghton Mifflin Company

The Grapes of Wrath
by John Steinbeck, Penguin Group

Great White Lie: Slavery, Emancipation and Changing Racial Attitudes
by Jack Gratus, Monthly Review Press

The Harder We Run: Black Workers Since the Civil War
by William Hamilton Harris, Oxford University Press

Home: Social Essays
by Amiri Baraka (LeRoi Jones), William Morrow Publishing Group

I Know Why the Caged Bird Sings
by Maya Angelou, Bantam Books

The Imitation of Christ
by Thomas à Kempis, Hendrickson Publishers, Inc.

Initiation
by Elisabeth Haich, Aurora Press, Inc.

In Search of Our Mother's Gardens
by Alice Walker, Sagebrush Education Resources

Interesting People: Black American History Makers
by George L. Lee, McFarland & Company, Inc.,
Publishers

I Shall Not Be Moved
by Maya Angelou, Random House Publishing Group

James Baldwin: The Legacy
Edited by Quincy Troupe, Simon & Schuster

*Kabbalah: A Definitive History of the Evolution,
Ideas, Leading Figures, and Extraordinary
Influence of Jewish Mystics*
by Gersham G. Scholem, Penguin Group

Life After Life
by Raymond A. Moody, Jr., M.D.

The Life and Words of Martin Luther King, Jr.
by Ira Peck, Sagebrush Education Resources

Life as Carola
by Joan Grant, Ariel Press

Linda Goodman's Sun Signs
by Linda Goodman, Bantam Doubleday Dell
Publishing Group

*Makes Me Wanna Holler: A Young Black Man in
America*
by Nathan McCall, Random House Publishing Group

The Meaning of Masonry
by W. L. Wilmshurst, Nu Vision Publications

Moby Dick
by Herman Melville, Dover Publications

Monster: The Autobiography of an L.A. Gang Member
by Sanyika Shakur, Sagebrush Education Resources

Music of Black Americans: A History
by Eileen Southern, W.W. Norton & Company, Inc.

Mysticism
by Evelyn Underhill

Native Son
by Richard Wright, HarperCollins Publishers

Nature, Man and Woman
by Alan W. Watts, Knopf Publishing Group

No Man Is an Island
by Thomas Merton, Shambhala Publications, Inc.

*Nostradamus: The Millennium & Beyond: the Prophecies
to 2016*
by Peter Lorie, Liz Greene, Simon & Schuster

One Hundred Years of Solitude
by Gabriel Garcia Márquez, HarperCollins Publishers

The Phenomenon of Man
by Teilhard de Chardin, HarperCollins Publishers

Ponder on This: A Compilation
by Alice A. Bailey, Lucis Publishing Company

The Practical Encyclopedia of Natural Healing
by Mark Bricklin, Rodale Press, Incorporated

ıe Prince
•y Niccolò Machiavelli, Bantam Classics

Psychedelic Experience—A Manual Based on the Tibetan Book of the Dead
by Timothy Leary, Ph.D., Ralph Metzner, Ph.D., and Richard Alpert, Ph.D., Carol Publishing Group

The Psychic Realm: What Can You Believe?
by Naomi A. Hintze and J. Gaither Pratt, Ph.D., Random House Publishing

A Raisin in the Sun
by Lorraine Hansberry, Knopf Publishing Group

Roots: The Saga of an American Family
by Alex Haley, Doubleday Publishing

Savage Inequalities: Children in America's Schools
by Jonathan Kozol, HarperCollins Publishers

Secret Splendor
by Charles Earnest Essert, Philosophical Library, Incorporated

Serving Humanity: A Compilation
by Alice A Bailey, Lucis Publishing Company

Sisterhood Is Powerful: Anthology of Writings from The Women's Liberation Movement
by Robin Morgan, Knopf Publishing Group

The Souls of Black Folk
by W. E. Burghardt DuBois, Simon & Schuster

State of the World Atlas
by Michael Kidron and Ronald Segal, Simon &
Schuster

Teachings of the Buddha
by Jack Kornfield, Shambhala Publications, Inc.

Telepathy and the Etheric Vehicle
by Alice A Bailey, Lucis Publishing Company

Thoughts and Meditations
by Kahlil Gibran, Carol Publishing Group

*The Tibetan Book of the Dead: Or, the After-Death
Experience on the Bardo Plane, according to Lama
Kazi Dawa-Sandup's English Renderings*
by W. Y. Evans-Wentz and Karma Glin-Pa, Oxford
University Press

Tropic of Cancer
by Henry Miller, Grove/Atlantic, Inc.

The Visionary Poetics of Allen Ginsberg
by Allen Ginsberg and Paul Portuges, Ross Erikson

Wisdom of Insecurity
by Alan Wilson Watts, Random House Publishing
Group

*Zen and the Art of Motorcycle Maintenance: An
Inquiry into Values*
by Robert M. Pirsig, HarperCollins Publishers

Quick Facts Timeline

1968–1971

September 1968: Tupac's mother, Afeni Shakur, joins the New York Black Panther Party.

April 1969: Afeni is arrested and charged with three hundred counts of conspiracy to bomb several public areas in New York City. While out on bail, Afeni gets pregnant by a party member other than her husband, Lumumba.

February 1971: Afeni's bail is revoked while she is pregnant and she is sent to the Women's House of Detention in Greenwich Village.

June 16, 1971: Shortly after his mother is acquitted on bombing charges, Tupac Amaru Shakur is born in New York.

1975–1983

Tupac's family shuttles between the Bronx and Harlem, at times living in shelters.

September 1983: Afeni enrolls young Tupac in the 127th Street Ensemble, a Harlem theater group. In his first performance, Tupac plays Travis in *A Raisin in the Sun*.

1984

June: The Shakur family moves to Baltimore. Tupac writes his first rhyme, using the name MC New York.

September: Tupac is enrolled at the Baltimore School for the Arts, where he studies ballet and acting.

1988

June: Tupac moves to Marin City, California, with his sister Sekyiwa. They stay with friends until Afeni can raise enough money to join them.

August: Mutulu Shakur, Tupac's stepfather, is sentenced to sixty years in prison for his involvement in a 1981 armored-car robbery.

1990

Tupac joins Digital Underground as a roadie and back-up dancer.

1991

January 3: Tupac makes his recording debut on Digital Underground's *This Is an E.P. Release*.

October 17: Tupac is stopped by two Oakland police officers for jaywalking and is subsequently beaten and arrested by the officers.

November 12: *2Pacaplypse Now* is released.

November 12: Tupac files a $10 million lawsuit against the Oakland Police Department for alleged police brutality following the arrest for jaywalking.

1992

January 17: Tupac makes his movie debut as the psychotic character Bishop in Ernest Dickerson's *Juice*.

April 11: Teenager Ronald Ray Howard, shoots a Texas state trooper. Howard's attorney claims Tupac's lyrics on *2Pacalypse Now*, which was in his client's tape deck, incited him to kill.

August 22: Tupac has an altercation with old acquaintances in Marin City, California. A six-year-old bystander is shot in the head. Tupac's stepbrother,

Mopreme, is arrested but released due to lack of evidence.

September 22: Tupac is publicly denounced by Vice President Dan Quayle.

1992: Suge Knight and Dr. Dre form Future Shock Records. A friend suggests the name Death Row Records, because everyone on the label has had run-ins with the law.

1992: Death Row's first album, *The Chronic,* by Dr. Dre, is released.

1993

February 1: *Strictly 4 My Niggaz* is released and eventually goes platinum.

March 13: Tupac has a fight with a limo driver, David DeLeon, in the parking lot of Fox Studios after a taping of *In Living Color.* DeLeon accuses Tupac of using drugs in the car. Tupac is arrested but the charges are dropped.

April 5: Tupac is arrested in Lansing, Michigan, for taking a swing at a local rapper with a baseball bat during a concert. He is sentenced to ten days in jail.

July 23: John Singleton's *Poetic Justice,* starring Tupac and Janet Jackson, is released.

September: Death Row's second album, *Doggystyle* by Snoop Dogg, is released.

October 31: Tupac is arrested for allegedly shooting two off-duty Atlanta police officers whom he says were harassing a black motorist.

November 18: Nineteen-year-old Ayanna Jackson, to whom Tupac was introduced four days earlier in a New York nightclub, Nell's, claims to have been sodomized and sexually abused by Tupac and three of his friends.

December: John Singleton is forced by Columbia Pictures to drop Tupac from Singleton's next movie, *Higher Learning.*

1994

March 10: Tupac is sentenced to fifteen days in a Los Angeles jail for punching out director Allen Hughes. Hughes and his brother, Albert, had dropped Tupac from *Menace II Society.*

March 23: Tupac stars as Birdie, a troubled drug dealer, in *Above the Rim.* The soundtrack album features the song "Pour Out a Little Liquor," recorded by Tupac's group, Thug Life.

September 7: Two Milwaukee teens murder a police officer and say Tupac's lyrics from *2Pacalypse Now* inspired them.

November 30: In the wee hours of the morning, Tupac is shot five times and robbed of over $40,000 worth of jewelry in the lobby of a Times Square recording studio. Tupac checks himself out of the hospital less than three hours after surgery.

December: Tupac is acquitted of sodomy and weapons charges but is found guilty of sexual abuse.

1995

February 14: Tupac is sentenced to four and a half years in a maximum security prison for sexual abuse. He immediately begins serving his time on New York's Rikers Island.

March 8: Tupac is transferred to Clinton Correctional Facilities in Dannemora, New York, a maximum-security penitentiary.

April: Tupac's third album, *Me Against the World,* debuts at number one on *Billboard*'s pop chart. The album goes double platinum in seven months, all while he was in prison.

April 29: Tupac marries his longtime girlfriend, Keisha Morris, in a jailhouse wedding performed by a justice of the peace.

April: In a *VIBE* interview from jail, Tupac renounces

the "Thug Life" persona and commits himself to positive work. He also implicates Biggie Smalls, Sean "Puffy" Combs, Andre Harrell, his close friend Randy "Stretch" Walker, and others in his November 1994 shooting.

August: In *VIBE* magazine Biggie, Puffy, and Harrell claim they had no connection to Tupac's shooting.

October: Death Row Records CEO Suge Knight posts $1.4 million bond to release Tupac, who immediately flies to L.A., signs with Death Row, and begins recording *All Eyez on Me*.

November 30: Exactly one year after Tupac's shooting, Randy "Stretch" Walker is murdered execution-style in Queens, New York.

1996

February: In *VIBE,* Tupac suggests he was sleeping with Biggie's wife, Faith Evans. She vehemently denies the stories.

February 13: Tupac's Death Row debut release, *All Eyez on Me*, is rap's first double CD.

February 28: After two and a half years of dealing with a murder charge, Snoop Dogg is found not guilty of all charges but one. The jury is deadlocked on the charge of voluntary manslaughter.

March 29: Words are exchanged and a gun is pulled when Death Row and BadBoy employees face off after the Soul Train Awards in Los Angeles.

April 25: *All Eyez on Me* goes quintuple platinum.

May: Tupac and Snoop Dogg release *2 of Amerikaz Most Wanted*. In the video are caricatures of Biggie and Puffy, and it depicts their punishment for setting up Tupac.

June: Dr. Dre leaves Death Row and relinquishes his half of the label he helped found with Suge Knight in 1992. Dre then starts his own label, Aftermath, with Interscope.

June 4: Death Row releases Tupac's "Hit 'Em Up," a dis rap that targets Biggie, Puffy, and Mobb Deep.

September 4: Tupac returns to New York for the MTV Music Awards and gets into a scuffle.

September 7: After leaving the Mike Tyson–Bruce Seldon fight in Las Vegas in Suge Knight's car, Tupac is shot four times in the chest by an assailant in a white Cadillac. Suge escapes with a minor injury. Shakur is rushed to University Medical Center, where he undergoes surgery, including the removal of his right lung.

September 9: Metro Police and about twenty friends and fans of Shakur are in an altercation over what police called a "misunderstanding." No one is arrested.

September 11: A Compton man who police said was associated with the Crips is shot to death while sitting in his car, the first in a series of gang-related murders. Police begin investigating possible connections to Tupac's shooting.

September 13: After several attempts to revive him, Tupac Amaru Shakur is pronounced dead at 4:03 P.M. At approximately 7:00 P.M., an autopsy is performed on the body that leads to the finding of homicide. At approximately 9:00 P.M., Tupac's body is released to Davis Mortuary and cremated.

September 14: Tupac's remains are given to his mother, Afeni Shakur, who leaves Las Vegas the same day and has yet to return.

October 23: Suge Knight is sent to jail for a parole violation in connection with the September 7 beating of Orlando Anderson at the MGM Grand in Las Vegas.

November 5: Just short of two months after Tupac's death, Death Row releases *The Don Killuminati: The 7 Day Theory* by Makaveli, a.k.a. Tupac Shakur.

November 13: Yafeu Fula, a member of the Outlawz and the only witness who claims to be able to visually identify Tupac's killer, is shot once in the head and killed in the hallway of his girlfriend's housing project in Orange, New Jersey.

November 15: Orlando Anderson testifies that Suge Knight did not assault him, but instead tried to break up the fight. He later says he lied on the stand about Suge's involvement because he was in fear of his life.

November 20: An Arkansas woman wins $16.6 million lawsuit against Tupac's estate after being paralyzed from a gunshot at a 1993 Tupac concert in a Pine Bluff, Arkansas, nightclub. The ruling is later overturned because Tupac's estate didn't have an opportunity to present a defense. She later appealed and settled for $2 million.

1997

January 29: Tupac Shakur appears in Vondie Curtis Hall's independent film *Gridlock'd*. Death Row releases the *Gridlock'd* sound track.

February 14: Suge Knight and lawyer David Kenner are sued by the American Express credit card company for unpaid bills totaling $1.67 million.

February 28: Suge Knight is sentenced to nine years, with one year's time served in prison for violating his 1995 probation.

March 9: Biggie Smalls is killed after being shot five times while sitting in the passenger seat of a Suburban after attending a Soul Train Music Awards party in Los Angeles.

March 27: Jacques Agnant, a.k.a. Nigel, one of the co-defendants in the 1994 sex abuse case against Tupac Shakur, files a $200 million libel suit against Tupac's estate for wrongfully stating that the lyrics in the track "Against All Odds" portrayed him as a police informant.

April 21: Death Row sues Tupac's estate for $7.1 million, demanding reimbursement for money allegedly advanced to him. The Shakur estate then files a countersuit for $17 million, claiming that Death Row failed to pay royalties to Tupac.

May: Suge Knight is transferred to the California Men's Colony in San Luis Obispo, to serve out his nine-year sentence. He is later moved to the Mule Creek Penitentiary for the remainder of his sentence.

June 3: Snoop Dogg is sued by his former manager, Sharitha Knight, estranged wife of Suge. She claims that she is owed her 20 percent commission of Snoop's earnings.

August 4: C. Delores Tucker files a $10 million lawsuit against Tupac's estate. Included in the suit are more than one hundred media outlets. She claims that Tupac's lyrics about her in two songs on *All Eyez On Me* defamed her character. The suit was later thrown out of court.

September: Afeni Shakur starts the Tupac Amaru Shakur Foundation in Atlanta, Georgia.

September 8: Tupac's poetry becomes the subject of scholarly debate at the University of California at Berkeley, where one hundred students sign up to study the poetry.

September 10: Orlando Anderson files a lawsuit against Tupac's estate. He claims that he suffered physical injuries and severe emotional and mental distress after the fight with Tupac on September 7, 1996.

September 16: Afeni Shakur counters Orlando's suit and files a wrongful-death lawsuit against him.

October 10: Tupac appears in the movie *Gang Related*. Death Row releases the *Gang Related* sound track.

November 25: Afeni Shakur releases the double album

R U Still Down Remember Me? on Amaru Records. The album sold more than four million copies.

November 14: Puffy begins the "No Way Out" Tour. He decides not to visit Los Angeles in light of Biggie's murder.

December 10: A lawsuit by Tupac Shakur's biological father, William Garland, claiming half of his son's assets, is denied. He later appeals and settles out of court for a total of $890,000.

1998

January: Interscope Records, at the direction of parent company Seagrams, decides to sever ties with Death Row. Priority immediately steps in as a replacement distributor.

January 9: The University of Wyoming offers a course for seventy-seven students that focuses on Tupac Shakur's life, music, films, and poetry.

January 15: Snoop Dogg reveals to a Long Beach newspaper his plans to leave Death Row. He claims Death Row has lost direction and that he fears for his life.

March 12: No Limit signs Snoop Dogg. Death Row agrees to sell Snoop's contract for a six-figure amount and future profit sharing of Snoop releases.

April 2: A R&S Antiques Inc. sues the estate of Tupac Shakur for $93,000. They claim that Tupac ran up a tab for jewelry and never paid for it.

May 30: Orlando Anderson is killed in a shootout at a Compton car wash that left two others dead in what is believed to be a dispute over money.

July 7: A judgment against the estate of Tupac Shakur for $210,000 is awarded to a Georgia state deputy sheriff shot by Tupac in 1993.

August 25: Tupac is remembered in a stage version of his life, *Judgment Day and the Search for the Invisible Man.*

November 24: *2Pac's Greatest Hits* is released by Amaru Records. The double album sold over nine million copies.

1999

April 21: An investigation begins into Suge Knight's connection with Biggie Smalls's death.

July: The Tupac Amaru Shakur Foundation begins the first summer session of PACamps with twenty campers.

September: In a statement of unity, Tupac's mother, Afeni Shakur, and Biggie's mother, Voletta Wallace, come together at the MTV Music Awards to present an award.

October: *The Rose that Grew from Concrete,* a book of Tupac's unpublished poetry, is published by MTV Books/Pocket Books.

December 15: Amaru Records releases the album *Still I Rise* by Tupac and the Outlawz.

2000

November: Amaru Records releases the audio version of *The Rose that Grew from Concrete* with various artists' and actors' interpretations of Tupac's poetry.

2001

March 27: Amaru Records releases Tupac's double album *Until the End of Time.* It features video footage of Tupac in the studio.

August 6: Suge is freed from prison after serving five years of a nine-year sentence for a parole violation. He had been jailed for participating in the beating of Orlando Anderson in Las Vegas.

2002

November: *Better Dayz,* the third album of Tupac's music on Amaru Records, is released.

2003

November 4: The movie *Tupac: Resurrection* is released by Paramount/MTV Films. The coffee-table book version of the movie is also released by Altria Books.

2004

February 19: Ratethemusic.com reports that Snoop Dogg credited the late Tupac Shakur for saving his marriage to wife Shantay Taylor. After hitting fame in the early 1990s, he considered breaking up with his then girlfriend Taylor, but Tupac stepped in. "That's your son's mother," Snoop said Pac told him. "You love her—she's the only one who's gonna love you." The couple got married in 1997, and have three children.

June 15: The movie *Tupac: Resurrection* is released in stores in DVD and VHS formats.

July 2: Tupac's half brother Mopreme Shakur becomes the newest member of Mob Life Records.

December 27: Tupac Shakur gains his third posthumous *Billboard* 200 chart-topper as *Loyal to the Game* enters the *Billboard* album chart at number one. The set, which sold 330,000 copies in the United States according to Nielsen SoundScan, became Tupac's fifth number one on the tally.

2005

March: Suge Knight, co-founder of Death Row, is ordered to pay $107 million to former business partner Lydia Harris.

June 11: The Tupac Amaru Shakur Center for the Arts celebrates its Garden Grand Opening in Stone Mountain, Georgia.

June 26: Just days after Tupac Shakur was gunned down, a security boss for his record label vowed to get his Brooklyn-born rap rival Notorious B.I.G. in retaliation, a witness tells a federal jury. "In a nutshell, Reggie [Wright Jr., then security chief for Death Row Records] told me: 'We're gonna get those motherfu**ers who downed 'Pac. . . . Biggie and his crew . . . we're gonna get 'em,'" Tupac's former bodyguard Kevin Hackie said.

December 16: Adrian Brody reportedly still cherishes the bit of graffiti "bombing" he did as a Queens teen with Tupac Shakur. "If I had more talent, I probably would have done more," he tells *Mass Appeal* magazine.

2006

January 13: Jimmy James Johnson punches Dr. Dre at the *VIBE* Awards and then is allegedly stabbed by G-Unit/Aftermath artist Young Buck, who pleads not guilty to assault charges.

January 15: Johnson tells police that Suge Knight paid him $5,000 to punch Dr. Dre as he accepted his Lifetime Achievement Award. Suge said he had nothing to do with the assault.

March 27: A Los Angeles judge threatens to take control of Suge Knight's assets, including Death Row Records, after the rap mogul neglected to pay off a multimillion-dollar debt.

April 1: Suge Knight skips a court-ordered appearance at a hearing about his assets, allowing a judge to decide whether a receiver will take control of Death Row Records.

April 16: *The Las Vegas Review Journal* reports that Tupac Shakur's sister, Sekyiwa "Set" Shakur, and aunt, Gloria "Glo" Cox, were among family members who attended the unveiling of the rapper's wax likeness at Madame Tussaud's Wax Museum in Las Vegas. His mother, Afeni, sent a statement thanking the museum for the honor, adding that she was still unable to visit Las Vegas, where the rap star was slain in September 1996.

April 16: The late Tupac Shakur is honored in the video for "When Ure Hero Falls," the first single from *The Rose, Vol. 2: Music Inspired by Tupac's Poetry*.

September 13: The tenth anniversary of Tupac Amaru Shakur's death.

Sources

Websites

www.2paclegacy.com
www.alleyezonme.com
www.hitemup.com
www.mtv.com
www.rollingstone.com
www.tasf.org
www.thugz-network.com
www.tupacfans.com
www.tupacnet.org
www.tupac-online.com

Books

2Pac Lives: the Death of Makaveli / The Resurrection of Tupac Amaru (Volume 1) by Drah Cenedive
Afeni Shakur: Evolution of a Revolutionary by Jasmine Guy
Back in the Day: My Life and Times With Tupac Shakur by Darrin Keith Bastfield
Dead or Alive: The Mystery of Tupac Shakur, the Alive Theories by John Doe
Holler If You Hear Me: Searching for Tupac Shakur by Michael Eric Dyson
Inside a Thug's Heart by Angela Ardis, Tupac Shakur
The Killing of Tupac Shakur by Cathy Scott
LAbyrinth: A Detective Investigates the Murders of Tupac Shakur and Notorious B.I.G., the Implication of Death

Row Records' Suge Knight, and the Origins of the Los
Angeles Police Scandal by Randall Sullivan
Rebel for the Hell of It: The Life of Tupac Shakur by
Armond White
The Rose That Grew from Concrete by Tupac Shakur
Thru My Eyes: Thoughts on Tupac Shakur in Pictures and
Words by Gobi
Tough Love: Cultural Criticism & Familial Observations on
the Life and Death of Tupac Shakur (Black Words Series)
by Michael Datcher (Editor)
Tupac: A Thug Life by Sam Brown
Tupac: Resurrection by Tupac Shakur, Jacob Hoye (Editor)
Tupac Shakur by Quincy Jones, VIBE magazine
Tupac Shakur (Rock Music Library) by Nathan Olson
Tupac Shakur (They Died Too Young) by Heather Forkos
The Tupac Shakur Collection by Tupac Shakur

DVD

Above the Rim (1994), New Line Home Video
Biggie & Tupac: The Story Behind the Murder of Rap's
Biggest Superstar (2002), Razor & Tie
Bullet (1996), New Line Home Video
Gang Related (1997), MGM
Gridlock'd (1997), Polygram USA
Juice (1992), Paramount
Poetic Justice (1993), Sony Pictures
Thug Immortal—The Tupac Shakur Story (1998), Xenon
Tupac—Live at the House of Blues (UMD Mini For PSP)
(1996), Eagle Vision USA
Tupac—Resurrection (2003), Paramount
Tupac Shakur—Before I Wake (2001), Xenon
Tupac Shakur—Thug Angel (The Life of an Outlaw)
(2002), Image Entertainment
Tupac: Hip Hop Genius (2005), Chrome Dreams Video
Tupac: Words Never Die (2005), Fieldstone Entertainment

Bibliography

Prologue: Death Around the Corner
Nuthin But a G Thing. Gangsta Rap: Culture and Commerce of Gangsta Rap, Columbia University Press

Chapter One: Part-Time Mutha
Afeni Shakur: Evolution of a Revolutionary by Jasmine Guy, Altria
Back in the Day: My Life and Times with Tupac Shakur, by Darin Keith Bastfield, De Capo Press

Chapter Two: Rebel of the Underground
VH1 Biography www.vh1.com
www.ybfree.com
Thug Angel, Tupac Shakur feature-length documentary (Image Entertainment). Composed score for film starring Tupac Shakur, Notorious B.I.G., Treach, Shock G, Snoop Dogg, Quincy Jones, Rashida Jones, and others. Produced by Quincy Delight Jones III (DVD)

Chapter Three: I Get Around
Tupac vs. Oakland Police Court Documents
Thug Angel, Tupac Shakur feature-length documentary (Image Entertainment). Composed score for film starring Tupac Shakur, Notorious B.I.G., Treach, Shock G, Snoop Dogg, Quincy Jones, Rashida Jones, and others. Produced by Quincy Delight Jones III (DVD)

Chapter Four: Keep Ya Head Up

The Rose that Grew From Concrete by Tupac Shakur

Tupac Resurrection: In his own words: Home movies, photographs, and recited poetry illustrate the life of Tupac Shakur, one of the most beloved, revolutionary, and volatile hip-hop MCs of all time. Director Lauren Lazin, Amaru Entertainment

Chapter Five: Me Against the World

Wounded Rapper Gets Mixed Verdict in Sex-Abuse Case, Richard Perez-Pena, *The New York Times*, December 1, 1994

Keisha Morris Profile, Rap News Network, 10/4/2004 from F.E.D.S Volume 2 Issue # 5

Alleymezone.com

Davy D Radio Interview KMEl Radio

VIBE magazine

Chapter Six: California Love

Does Sugar Bear Bite, by Lynn Hirschburg (*New York Times*), Published: January 14, 1996

Tupac Interview, Tabitha Soren, MTV, October 27, 1995

2Pac, Interview, KMEL's Westside Radio Program, April 19, 1996, transcribed by Davey D

Tupac Interview, conducted by Master T for MTV

Jurors Accquit Rap Musician in Murder Case, *The New York Times*, Published: February 22, 1996

Chapter Seven: Hail Mary

Barry's Boxing Center Website: www.barrysboxingcenter.com

Las Vegas Sun, news article

VIBE magazine

The Killing of Tupac, by Cathy Scott, Hunington Press Publishing

Got Your Back: Protecting Tupac in the World of Gangsta Rap by Frank Alexander

Chapter Eight: Life of an Outlaw

www.Alleymezone.com

Tupac Resurrection: In his own words: Home movies, photographs, and recited poetry illustrate the life of Tupac Shakur, one of the most beloved, revolutionary, and volatile hip-hop MCs of all time. Director Lauren Lazin, Amaru Entertainment

Billboard magazine

Associated Press, Gina Longo Story

Los Angeles Times, Gina Longo Story

New Yorker magazine article

The Killing of Tupac, by Cathy Scott, Hunington Press Publishing

Chapter Nine: Blasphemy

CNN Saturday Morning News, Reporter: Who Killed Tupac Shakur?, Aired September 14, 2002, 07:45 ET

Gangsta Label Accuses Time Warner of Racketeering, by Mark Landler, Published: August 19, 1995

Rebel for the Hell of It: The Life of Tupac Shakur by Armond White

Rap Cointelpro Part VI: A Civil War Within Hip-Hop: www.blackelectorate.com

Chapter 10: How Long Will They Mourn Me?

Pac's death devastates rap star, T.I. "not ever going to be the same," by Sonia Murray, *The Atlanta Journal-Constitution,* Published: 05/07/06

Rap Cointelpro: Tupac Shakur by Quincy Jones

LAbyrinth: A Detective Investigates the Murders of Tupac Shakur and Notorious B.I.G., the Implication of Death Row Records' Suge Knight, and the Origins of the Los Angeles Police Scandal by Randall Sullivan

The Rose that Grew from Concrete by Tupac Shakur

www.thuglife.com

DATE DUE